EQUINE JOURNEYS

JOURNEYS

The British Horse World

(left) One of a pair of hundred-foot-high horse heads, known as The Kelpies, soaring above the landscape at Helix Park, Falkirk. In Scottish folklore, the mythical Kelpies haunt rivers and streams, granting their rider with the strength and stamina of more than ten horses. Designed by sculptor Andy Scott, this work was completed in 2013 and sits beside the Forth and Clyde Canal

Hossein Amirsadeghi

EQUINE JOURNEYS

The British Horse World

TransGlobe Publishing

TransGlobe Publishing Limited
5 Fleet Place
London EC4M 7RD
United Kingdom

info@tgpublishingltd.com
www.tgpublishingltd.com

First published by
TransGlobe Publishing Limited

© 2018 TransGlobe Publishing

Text and captions
© 2018 TransGlobe Publishing

© Photographs by Hossein Amirsadeghi

Distributed worldwide
Thames & Hudson Ltd.
181A High Holborn
London, WC1V 7QX
United Kingdom

www.thamesandhudson.com

ISBN: 978-0-9935951-0-3

British Library Cataloguing-in-Publication Data
A catalogue record for this book is available
from the British Library

Designed by Struktur Design Limited
Printed and bound in China

Contents

Equine Journeys

Hossein Amirsadeghi

Every journey has both a beginning and an ending. Yet my adventures in exploring creativity's bounds while extending the reach of the enigmatic in visual and narrative form seem to know no beginnings or endings. Hence *Equine Journeys: The British Horse World*, a book dedicated to the beauty of *Equus* and Britain's horse environment.

Why Britain?
Apart from the fact that these small islands have always been at the vanguard of equine history, there are nineteen million British 'equestrian consumers' with a range of associated interests (nearly a third of the country's population). There are 2.7 million active horse riders, 60 per cent of whom take part in some form of non-affiliated competition. The average annual spend per liveried horse is £4,000 in Britain today, with a million equines of one sort or another scattered across the country among half a million horse-owning households, not counting professional breeders. A quarter of a million horse lovers participate annually in professional competitions, everything from internationally renowned races at Ascot and Aintree to

local pony clubs and gymkhanas; from polo clubs and countryside hunts to endurance challenges like the Cairngorm 100 in Scotland. The British horse-racing, breeding and eventing realm is a multi-billion-pound business, reputedly the second-largest employer in the countryside after the farming industry. And, contrary to most other enterprises in Britain today, three-quarters of riders and those engaged in the livery trade are female.

The estimated value of riding lessons in the United Kingdom alone is £500 million a year, with a spend of £560 million on everything from clothing, hats and body protectors to equine publications. The British equestrian industry's output (from consumer businesses such as tack, feed, livery yards, riding schools, farriers, saddlers, specialist vets, etc.) is estimated at £4.5 billion a year, employing a quarter of a million people. Eleven million Brits have some interest in the horse industry, and more than six million visit the races each year. An increasing number from all backgrounds invest in horseflesh through direct purchases or as part of syndicates. In 2018, seven thousand breeders had twenty thousand horses in training. The horse business is therefore a large contributor to the country's economy and to its social fabric, especially in rural areas. Yet politically, this economic and social mass is underrepresented, punching well below its weight.

Horses have been an integral part of the rural landscape of the British Isles since time immemorial, helping to enhance stewardship of the land and perpetuate customs and traditions. The contemporary rise in eco-tourism, along with urban escapism into the countryside (2015 saw three million people taking riding holidays in Britain), are factors in horse-related government policy and on horse-federation planning agendas. Not to forget increasing numbers of global racing enthusiasts attending the annual equine calendar. Godolphin, Juddmonte and Shadwell are just a few of the major foreign-owned studs which have grown in size and success over the last quarter-century; equine inward investment has been on the rise from as far afield as China, the Middle East, Russia and Japan. Then there's the bloodstock trade spearheaded by Tattersalls, auctioneers with a £350 million turnover in 2017.

To undertake purposeful endeavour in such a vast field as the world of the British horse should make one think twice under the best of circumstances, especially if one is no expert. Such a daunting challenge is further amplified when confronting a close-knit fraternity often suspicious of outsiders. *The Arabian Horse*, my previous equine adventure (first published in 1998), did help to open doors. Nevertheless, to feel oneself firmly in the saddle, so to speak, involved not a little perseverance and some heavy horse trading. You can lead a horse to water, as the expression goes ... But enough equine metaphors.

(right) The shadow of the photographer observing Lady Martha Sitwell and a fellow horsewoman gathering hay for their horses at Kirtlington Manor Park stables after a gruelling four-hour winter cross-country ride with the Bicester Hunt near Oxford

The intellectual grounding for lifelong passions is often traceable back to its origins; mine was an early fascination with *Equus*, going back to part of my childhood spent in a dingy library. Sent as a young boy for an education at a Kent boarding school, I must have needed serious training or taming; to be broken in, as it were. The library itself was small with a limited selection of books, overwhelmed by the presence of a huge discoloured Chesterfield which had seen better days the century before. It suited my purposes, though, especially as other pupils seemed to care little for the bookworm privileges thus afforded. I grew fond of my time spent among the musty-smelling, well-thumbed volumes on history and war that dominated the shelves. Far from my Persian origins with nobody to shepherd my literary tastes (or anything else for that matter), I settled upon a routine of escaping reality by visiting such historical figures as Cyrus the Great, Alexander of Macedon, Julius Caesar, Napoleon and Wellington. These men, plus Boudicca (the only woman featured in my library books), were always pictured with their horses in dramatic poses both noble and arresting. At least it seemed that way in the pages of history, just as they and their minions intended it would. Imagine all that equine glamour pitted against the sensibilities of a boy stuck in a boring seaside town, with weekly obligatory swims in the cold, uninviting Thames Estuary the only other (unwelcome) distraction. I put the blame for my miserable enforced state at the feet of the ancient Spartans, with their unholy influence on nineteenth-century English educators. A great bunch of horsemen by the way, the Spartans.

Horses didn't change the world, or did they?
By the time I went up to university and indulged in a total immersion in history, I had determined that it was the rider (whether warrior or ploughman), more than any other personality or profession, who scripted history. Not so much in big brushstrokes but in smaller incremental steps. Little steps don't make it into the history books or the annals of national glory, of course; it's far easier to captivate the imagination with the Big Picture. Given the boundless power of the human imagination, it was easy for me to craft *Boy's Own* stories around these men (and some women) and their horses. Prodded by the *Histories*, for example, it was an easy next step to imagine Cyrus riding his white Nisean into battle, just as Herodotus described him: 'In front of the king went first a thousand horsemen, picked men of the Persian nation – then spearmen a thousand, likewise chosen troops, with their spearheads pointing towards the ground – next ten of the sacred horses called Nisaeans, all daintily caparisoned.'

The Nisean was the mount of nobility in ancient Persia, pulling the King of Kings' chariot. Given the absence of stirrups at the time, horsemanship and manageability had far more meaning than they do today. Cyrus is said to

(above) Lord of the Manor
Sir Humphry Wakefield
riding through the grounds
of Chillingham Castle,
Northumberland in the
dead of winter

have been so distraught at the drowning of his horse while attempting a water crossing that he had the river drained as punishment. Not to be outdone, Alexander's mythically beloved horse, Bucephalus (Oxhead), had a city named after him upon the horse's death in battle. Three-toed with a massive head (but of indeterminate height), Bucephalus' vestigial equine atavism became the lure for Julius Caesar's myth-making three centuries later. Caesar purposely bred three-toed, white horses which he used to embellish his own legend by claiming direct equine descent from Alexander. Marengo, Napoleon Bonaparte's Arabian, which he brought back from his Egyptian campaign, was the horse he loved most. The Emperor's iconic image painted by Jacques-Louis David is striking in that one is more taken by the horse than by the man. Copenhagen, Wellington's warhorse at Waterloo, was sired by a dam that was daughter to the appropriately named John Bull. A dark chestnut of mixed thoroughbred and Arabian blood, Copenhagen bore his master in the saddle for seventeen hours straight while the battle lasted, yet nearly killed the Duke after he dismounted, startled by his master's pat on the neck.

These great men rode to glory, or death, mounted on beautiful horses which helped to enhance their mythical personas. How could one not be mesmerised as a child by such tales of equine and human derring-do? After seeing the overwhelming statue of Boudicca atop her scythed chariot on a school outing to Westminster and the Houses of Parliament, I decided that women too rocked on horseback.

My introduction to the actual sport was no less dramatic but far more modest. I first mounted a horse in my early twenties, a black Arabian stallion with a mind of its own – or, as I was to learn later, out of its mind. The poor creature was put down after killing two pedestrians walking along a country lane. Forget the fear of that first ride; the exhilaration of losing control, of being swept away at what seemed unearthly speeds, was enough to get me hooked. But horsemanship is more than a weekend rider's fancy. It requires passion and commitment, something which (I've since learned) is instilled in serious horse people from an early age. How else would you expect someone to get up most days at unholy hours in all weather conditions to tend to a horse, feed it, muck out its stable and ride the animal into shape? The routines involved are very demanding on both time and resources. That's why I never became a horseman, one among many pursuits that have taken my fancy over the years, yet never come to full fruition.

What better way, then, to live such experiences with equivalent intensity (mixed in with a little craziness) than to make books on the subjects of one's fancy or fantasy? You get to live the full life cycle for a year while escaping the worst of the grind, and still enjoy the sublime and the indescribable that such real-life journeys offer. Translating those experiences for an audience, evoking the feelings and emotions engendered, is the job of the creator, which I hope to have realised in some measure through *Equine Journeys*.

Fast forward sixty-odd years and I find myself regenerating lost or dormant passions and producing books on subjects as varied as horse, hawk and hunter (not forgetting art, politics and strategy). Who can be mindful of such mundane matters as international affairs, local

(left) Yearlings grazing at Cowdray Estate near Midhurst, West Sussex

politics and pocketbook economics when confronted with *Equus luxuriosus*? Leave aside the malign majesty of money that reigns over any social order – the fifty million or hundred million, guineas people pay for thoroughbreds in the case of the horse world. Forget all that and drive through England's green and pleasant land during spring, summer, autumn and even winter. Dare to not be stopped in your tracks by the sight of horses grazing in a field beneath crimson sunsets; glimpsed over the crest of a hill shadowed by the mighty summer sun; encountered of an afternoon with a hacker riding down some lonely country lane mottled with splashes of white light filtering through beech, birch, lime, chestnut or majestic English oaks. Winter presents horses draped in blankets grazing in the sullen cold, drawn to the human presence each time you happen to stop for a chat. Watch a champion eventer take a death-defying leap over a high fence while riding through rough countryside. See a young woman jump over the moon at Badminton, or glimpse a jockey preening in outrageously colourful attire, having won a race on one or other of the sixty courses scattered across Britain, from Perth in Scotland to Newton Abbot in Devon. Any of these experiences inspire passion to spare. They all inspired me during my 9,000-mile journey making *Equine Journeys*.

Human history has been trail-blazed on the back of the horse, humanity's most important companion in the animal kingdom. Legend, myth, literature, poetry and art have symbolically elevated *Equus caballus* beyond mere figurative or narrative representation. Forget the aesthetic pleasure surrounding the vision of a prize stallion, the flutter of emotions engendered by a day spent at the races or indulging humanity's penchant for gambling, from which has arisen today's multi-billion-pound racing empires. The route of ideas and the movement of peoples across civilisations are predicated on the horse – it's simple really. The advent of the Agricultural and Industrial revolutions owed a great deal to our four-legged partners, to *horsepower*. Today, of course, there are no physical, material or war-fighting roles attributable to the horse. Where once battles were won and empires lost because of the quality of horses, today's horse is no longer of industrial or agricultural benefit to human beings. It has evolved in other directions, however, transformed for sport at the public level, and for personal indulgence in search of excellence at the private one.

Gambling on horses has existed since the time of their domestication. Chariot races were common throughout the Roman Empire, with large sums changing hands as powerful men challenged each other in political and sporting grudge matches. In England, large estates were won and lost on a single horse race wagered among the aristocracy in the seventeenth and eighteenth centuries at The Jockey Club in Newmarket. The kings Charles I and II

were particular enthusiasts, a tradition passed on within the British monarchy well into the twenty-first century. The frequent presence of betting shops in neighbourhoods up and down the country attests to a continued predilection for horse gambling. The social misery of gambling is well documented, yet we cheer the odd bet that makes history. In 1903, the Hermits, a five-man group of professional gamblers from the Salisbury Plain, made a winning bet of £250,000 on a horse called Hackler Pride; this was the equivalent of £10 million in today's money. The Jockey Club – Britain's largest commercial group, operating fifteen racecourses around the country – had a record-breaking year in 2017. Off-course betting turnover was £4.4 billion.

Setting aside equine sport and pleasure, the horse became humanity's companion-in-arms, privileged above all other animals in value and esteem. The Comte de Buffon, eighteenth-century polymath and naturalist, referred to the horse as 'the most noble conquest of mankind'. As symbols of power and beauty, nothing has come close. The horse predates humans by millions of years, with humanity's ancestors hunting proto-equine variations as food on the hoof. To such an extent that horses became extinct in the Americas ten thousand years ago, only to be reintroduced by the Spanish Conquistadors in the 1500s. The horse as we know it today evolved over 50 million years, first domesticated on the Eurasian steppes, where a sustainable monoculture was managed by nomadic tribes who drew nearly all their existential needs from the horse. The very same tribes would later leave fear and destruction in their wake while conquering much of the known world, coming as far as the heart of medieval Europe, collapsing empires and conquering all before them with their plentiful supply of steppe horses and skills as fearless warrior horsemen. Think Genghis Khan and his grandson Kublai; tremble at the memory of Tamerlane. I did. We were regaled as children with bedtime stories of the Mongol hoards' cruel and efficient war machine, told a thousand years after the destruction of Persianate lands and peoples. Those wild and mysterious steppe horses have long disappeared, made extinct by human hands.

Language and culture have spread on horseback too. Early admiration for this fierce, apparently untameable and inspiring animal set the tone for how horses would be regarded through the annals of cultural memory and centuries of visual history-making. Art, literature and poetry have glorified in the horse. The freedom embodied in riding at speed, the skills and challenges of horsemanship, the tenacity involved in training a wild horse, have contributed to myth and legend in all societies save for sub-Saharan cultures. While the horse may have been domesticated, tamed and corralled, humanity has fashioned some of its own more fanciful characteristics

on the equine's noble and loyal personality and freedom. Wild yet loyal, courageous yet so fragile, with up to a ton of horseflesh perched atop legs and hooves seemingly so frail, they have inspired the lyrics of many poets:

> With flowing tail, and flying mane,
> Wide nostrils never stretch'd by pain,
> Mouths bloodless to the bit and rein,
> And feet that iron never shod.
> And flanks unscarr'd by spur and rod,
>
> A thousand horse, the wild, the free,
> Like waves that follow o'er the free,
> Came thickly thundering on.

Lord Byron's 1819 *Mazeppa* was fashioned around myth posing as reality, in this case immortalising myths surrounding the seventeenth-century Ukrainian warrior-general Ivan Mazeppa. The lovelorn and luckless Mazeppa fell foul of his King, having fallen in love with and seduced the Queen. The hapless lover ended up strapped naked to the back of a wild horse and let loose in the wild as punishment. Lovers and horses are recurring themes around our cultural romance with the horse, accentuated by the real dramas of history.

Such romantic visions and visual records can be sustaining as one travels up and down Britain's motorway networks. Terrible weather, more bad weather, inaccessible places, useless detours and bad judgement calls can wear on a man's patience and passion. Perfectionism (the creative's primary disease) is its own worst enemy, yet great food for creative enterprise.

(below & opposite) Seasonal colour reflected on the highways and byways of the English countryside

Apart from meeting horses and greeting their keepers along the journey's divides, some of my most striking memories are of landscapes in both clement and cruel weather. Having lived in England on and off for sixty years, I'd never managed a closer look at the landscape than I experienced over the past twelve months. The delights of euphemistically termed AONBs (Areas of Outstanding Natural Beauty) can outpace a race against the best of the British horse. Horses are ubiquitous across the countryside, often hidden in plain sight in settings as brash and diffident as the Surrey Hills, South Downs, Cotswolds, Chiltern Hills, Malvern Hills, Norfolk and Suffolk coasts, Snowdonia, the Wye Valley, the Scottish Borders, Dartmoor, Exmoor, the North York Moors, the Northumberland coast and the Durham Dales. The civility, communal tranquillity, and passionate stewardship of land and traditions, along with the general equanimity of British country folk, impressed me as never before. Reflective of the equestrian fraternity as a whole, this mild-mannered tempo of English rural living is a world apart from urban norms. A first-time visitor could not be faulted for thinking the divides almost become tribal identifiers, with visible chasms in the expression of national ethos between inner-city inhabitants compared, say, to the Cotswolds, the Pennines or the South West. The West Country English seem a class apart; cultural passport controls would not be out of place when entering the Cotswolds. While the metropolitan mindset seems to be engaged in a constant battle for material ascendancy and survival, the English countryside is a peculiarly egalitarian commons, with pecking orders long defined by landed gentry, village and church, all overseen by the established aristocracy. Nowhere is this more evident than in the horsey realm, where everyone is treated with equal respect, from stable lads to work riders, jockeys to trainers to owners. Perhaps rigorous hard work and the entwining nature of horse culture set the norms – no-one is any better than their labour.

Meanwhile, weather is the joker in the pack. Expecting spring, I faced a bitterly cold April mist in Newmarket, out of which walked Sir Mark Prescott. One of Britain's most renowned thoroughbred trainers, Prescott is the owner of Heath House Stables, the oldest yard in what is Britain's pre-eminent horse-breeding region. He has an enviable record of nearly three thousand winners during a career spanning five decades. A confirmed bachelor at sixty-nine, Prescott is a figure of legend in the breeding world. He still arrives at the stable yard at the crack of dawn with no breaks or holidays. 'They'll know I've resigned my role if I'm not there at 6.15 a.m. sharp,' he says without jest. 'They can send for the knacker's cart!' A baronet expelled from Harrow as a teenager for putting a whoopee cushion on the preacher's seat on Founder's Day, Prescott went to work in the horse world, beginning at the bottom of the ladder mucking out stables. He broke his back two years later while riding and remained hospitalised for eighteen months, yet went on to obtain his trainer's licence in 1970. 'Life is to be lived fully' is the motto of the 3rd baronet, who loves hare coursing, cock- and bullfighting, hunting and any other country pursuits scorned or regarded as politically incorrect. As for his fearsome temper, the man whose lady friends are not permitted within 50 miles of his Newmarket stables can only say, 'I'm not so bad now.'

Although a pretty hardy, sometimes dour, no-nonsense group of professionals who eat, sleep and drink horses 24/7, trainers on the whole tend to keep to themselves. There's really no time to do or think anything but horses, Britain's leading hunt trainer Nicky Henderson

admits. 'We're quite boring in our habits,' the Lambourn-based Henderson confesses. In order to marry his long-time companion, he had to schedule the happy event according to the vagaries of the equine calendar, lest it get in the way of the work of winning races. The economics of the trainer's business are relentless and ruthless – you're only as good as the last year's winners. Lambourn itself couldn't be more different from Newmarket. The latter is in flat, uninspiring Suffolk landscape centred around a nondescript town, while Lambourn is far more laid back and surrounded by exceptionally beautiful rolling Berkshire countryside in which nestles a quaint little town. Some of these English hamlets, villages and picture-perfect smaller towns are a boon to any traveller.

This countryside has been shaped by both humans and horses. Watching early-morning equine displays of speed and agility at Newmarket's Warren Hill gallops, it's clear that the animals today bear no resemblance to those that helped fashion the country at large. Farm and draught horses were large, sturdy creatures fit for purpose, while these beauties are born and bred to speed with little room to spare for long-distance stamina – a point driven home on the car ride from Newmarket to the Suffolk coast in search of the rare Suffolk Punch. I happened upon some missing pages from the journey's equine history, spotting Sutton Hoo along the way. The site of major sixth- and seventh-century Anglo-Saxon archaeological finds, Sutton Hoo's treasure of gold artefacts is housed in the British Museum. For my purposes, the most interesting discovery was the ancient burial chamber of a young man with his horse. Deified by most ancient cultures, including Celtic and Germanic tribes, burials of horses were common from Palaeolithic times onwards. Herodotus mentions the custom among the Scythians, while Chinese emperors and warlords interred large numbers of sacrificial horses along with their dead masters.

The Sutton Hoo site, it transpired, had been occupied from the Neolithic period, sparking my imagination on this mystery tour traversing equine history, tracing the magic of the horse from the distant past to its present. I learned that the area's dark soil was used to grow large cabbages during the Iron Age. Seeing fields of cabbages in early spring's heavy mist triggered some imaginary time-travel, the click of my camera's lens conjuring up the long-dead young Suffolk warrior astride his horse, carrying his sword and his bow, in the time of the Kingdom of East Anglia. What did the animal look like? What was its name, its breed, its colour? How did the warrior come to die? Was there a wife? The camera's clicks captured her despair as she watched her warrior and his horse being covered by the soil of time. Pulling into a side road, I searched for poetic resonance and came upon Alfred, Lord Tennyson's verse:

> *Home they brought her warrior dead:*
> *She nor swooned, nor uttered cry:*
> *All her maidens, watching, said,*
> *'She must weep or she will die.'*

Evolution's cumulative layers of change shroud life's mundanities with thick layers of mystery, the source of much fantasy. Such emotions came to the fore at the sight of Achilles, a massive-headed, thick-necked, broad-shouldered Suffolk Punch stallion who is one of the few remaining sires of the breed. The leaden skies, muddy fields, heavy clod and uninspiring paddock provided background to the scene. Something about this primordial brew of horse and history held the attention, given that I had arrived by way of Sutton Hoo. One of the oldest breeds in Britain, the Suffolk Punch became the region's workhorse, but its sullen look born of idleness masked the creep of extinction. Achilles deserves a burial mound of his own, I have no doubt.

Across the country, I'd experienced another time-traveller's moment while visiting the Uffington White Horse atop the highest point in Oxfordshire. Racing a brilliant autumn sunset, I found the three-thousand-year-old hill where the stylised Iron Age piece of minimalist art is sketched across

(above) The author at work in the Scottish hills, and (left) a flat landscape in the Cotswolds

360 feet on a slope, its outline formed by deep trenches filled with crushed chalk. The stunning view of surrounding farmland and the hard climb to beat the setting sun with nothing and no-one to spoil the mood set the mind racing. Much is known about the site and its parallel hill fort located atop a higher knoll, but the magic of the moment forced me to sit a while and hazard the darkening sky, a cell phone my only source of light other than the onset of a lazy moon.

An eleventh-century Abingdon Abbey cartulary makes mention of 'The White Horse Hill'. The *Red Book of Hergest*, a medieval Welsh text, refers to the site in the fourteenth century. And eighteenth-century writers mention the seven-year ritual of scouring the White Horse to keep it trim and visible. Of the various theories I researched on the subject, the favourite is that of the 'solar horse', a reflection of pagan belief that the sun was carried across the sky on a horse. Even the heavens have their horse-racing calendar, it would seem, with the summer and winter solstices chasing one another other across the universe.

From pagan ritual to haunted castle, my equine magical mystery tour brought me to Chillingham Castle in Northumberland in the dead of winter to meet Sir Edward Humphry Tyrrell Wakefield, Bt, FRGS, 2nd baronet and guardian of all things British, traditional and aristocratic. Sir Humphry is a character cut from the colourful cloth of British history. An ex-soldier, adventurer and art connoisseur, he bought the eleventh-century castle in the 1980s, going on to refurbish the crumbling pile, which had been in his wife's family (the Greys) for centuries. Ghost stories abound at Chillingham and there's a brisk trade in visitors who come to tremble the night away, hoping (or not) to see, sense or hear the dead. Sir Humphry himself is fond of regaling the visitor with incidents involving ghosts past and present. A keen horseman even before he joined the 10th Royal Hussars, his rapid-fire stories from soldiering and polo days in the Middle East, adventures with horses, climbing Mount Everest or surviving a plane crash while on an Antarctic expedition don't leave the visitor much choice but to listen attentively. Sir Humphry's passions, his love of horsemanship since the age of three and his unabashed political incorrectness – unsolicited statements that would crash Notting Hill or Chelsea dinner parties in the click of a horse's hoof – reveal more about England's gentry than any amount of historical trivia.

(above) Arabian horses, black beauties incongruously at home in the Scottish Borders, far removed from their desert origins

From haunted castles to idyllic churchyards, *Equine Journeys* next took me to St Mary and St Peter's Church in Salcombe Regis, Devon to meet Mary King. The three-time world-champion eventer started her equine journey at the age of three in the very same churchyard in which I photographed Mary with her mother, the current verger. As it happens, Mary King's father was the verger of the church for many years, having retired from the Merchant Navy. The priest at the time kept two horses and a pony, thus allowing Mary the chance to learn to ride, becoming world champion three decades, and six Olympics, later.

One of the least expected delights in travelling the country to create *Equine Journeys* was the discovery of churchyards, magnificent havens of nature and spirituality originating from medieval through to Victorian times. Sanctuaries to dead souls and living flora, supporting several-hundred-year-old oak trees and even older yew trees, their quietude and sense of peace (reflecting the shade on a hot summer's afternoon) are in themselves worth all the effort involved in creating this book. The fascinating background to the poisonous yew trees brought the subject of pagan rituals back to my note-taking. The Devil himself is said to dance on chimneys if yew wood is burned. Other stories point to yew trees' churchyard locations as sites of the hermitages of early saints. Death, the daughter of Sleep and Night, has spawned twenty thousand church- and graveyards across Britain, six thousand of which are 'Living Churchyards', a project intended to allow natural ecosystems to survive and thrive. Acting as genetic banks, the common-or-garden church- or graveyard is remarkably rich in varying species under threat from modern land use and chemicals.

What was revealing about my traveller's role was witnessing the wide differences in cultural perceptions between Britain's urban majority and its rural population, more so among the large horsey community. The extraordinary vitriol of urbanites towards the traditional sport of fox hunting has had tempers on both sides at the boil since the 2004 Hunting Act banning the sport. The Beaufort, Bicester and Yeomanry hunts featured in the book were a revelation in how the horse is the mainstay of cultural traditions dating back centuries, not just for the satisfaction of the sporting nobility and landed gentry but across all sectors of the community. Ignorance plays a part in urban animosity to rural fox hunting, as does class prejudice; both sides have claims on the moral high ground. Yet coming face to face with a pack of purebred fox hounds whose pedigrees can be traced back several centuries is a sight to be remembered. It was the beauty, animal power and intelligence of these canines that caught my fancy more than the fashionable frills of the hunters.

From gentry to gentle folk, large country piles to small gypsy wagons, one of the more enjoyable aspects of creating *Equine Journeys* was meeting ordinary horse enthusiasts – riders, owners and the workers employed in the industry. A hard life is the lot of the groom or stable hand, yet enthusiasm is never in short supply. Poorly paid and worked hard, these young people possess an enviable purity of spirit.

Then there's the mom-and-pop duo running a small stud farm for rare species, devoting their lives to the survival of breeds such as the Highland, Exmoor or Dartmoor Pony, Cleveland Bay, or Welsh or Gypsy Cob. Missionary and part evangelist, these horse lovers expect little in return for their hard labour under trying circumstances except the good of their horses.

(left) Sarah Byrne readying her horse for the Bicester Hunt, while (above) a family set off on the Beaufort Hunt's first day, as the famed Beaufort Kennels' hounds (right) await the call of the hunt's Master

(above) Yeomanry Hunt
participants preparing to set
off in mid-morning winter
sunshine. Long-standing
etiquette accompanies
riders at every turn, with
traditions built into the
fabric of British hunt society

I'd been looking for the Gypsy Cob for months, trying to pin down travellers to profile for the book. There's the Appleby Fair in Cumbria at the beginning of every summer, but that's more of a jamboree for tens of thousands of Gypsies, travellers and fellow-travellers congregating to have a knees-up along with their animals. I wanted the genuine article and happened upon my profilees camped alongside the Kirtlington Park Polo Club in Oxfordshire of all places. Near as they were to the home of the Bicester Hunt, the irony was not lost on either side as we sat on the fence discussing class, traveller culture and fox hunting. Alex Fenton, a striking woman in her mid-thirties with auburn hair and piercing green eyes, could have been sourced by central casting. She'd chosen the lifestyle, she said, in preference to all others available to her. 'The feel of the hunters' horses galloping past always gives me a buzz,' she remarked as stragglers from the Bicester charged past trying to salvage their honour, each touching their riding hat to our kerbside travellers. 'Live and let live, I say,' Fenton's companion Jason Wood remarked as the dust settled. 'They're not pushing us out of their posh neighbourhoods.' 'A traveller is a cultural thing to a lot of people,' Fenton went on to observe. 'In this country we have Romany travellers, Irish travellers, then I suppose New Age travellers, who weren't born travellers but chose the lifestyle ... Then you've got the second generation: kids that have been on the road from the '70s when their parents were going to festivals ... The children have carried on and had children themselves.' A tree surgeon by profession (when it takes her fancy or as need commands), Fenton (and Wood too) were reflective of the civility inspired by shared equine values regardless of class or status.

Moving from the flat landscapes of Oxfordshire to the hills and crags of Dartmoor, where natural beauty and landscape make the work of a writer more difficult, try describing Dartmoor on a sunny autumn morning, a wild foal being cossetted by its mother in the shade of a tree next to a natural watering hole. The smell of autumn's wild moorland grasses, ferns and bushes; the almost-taste of rainwater reflecting the mid-morning sunlight off the water. The wonder of mother with child, a wild Dartmoor mare stretched out next to her bay foal, the camera's intrusion not worth bothering about. Closing the eyes for a moment to take it all in, sinking into the timeless landscape free from all burdens, free as the wild ponies.

The variety of British horse breeds is the by-product of their environment. Dartmoor, Exmoor, Shetlands, Highlands, Eriskay, Welsh Cob, Cleveland Bay, Suffolk Punch, Shire horse – all have developed over centuries to serve humanity's purposes. But their economic usefulness has run its course, the centre of equine attraction moving on from these traditional breeds to the new super-thoroughbreds. It's a long road through time from the verdant splendour of a Lambourn stable to the health of the Dartmoor pony and livelihood of small stakeholders like Joyce and Jacky Newbery. A hard-working mother-and-daughter team based on the outskirts of Exeter, the Newberys run a livery stable catering to the needs of the local community while running a breeding programme for pure-bred Dartmoor ponies in order to help sustain the species' long-term survival. A semi-feral breed owned and protected by Dartmoor Commoners, the ponies have roamed free on moorland since the Middle Ages. Used by tin miners and quarry workers in the past, the breed's population of thirty thousand wild ponies in the 1960s is today reduced to a mere thousand. 'It's important to keep the bloodlines going,' observed Joyce over a cup of tea in the small dining room of her modest home abutting the stables. The din of dogs vying for attention mixed with the pitter-

(below left to right) Essences captured on the journey, from a groom shaving a horse in Northamptonshire, to a rider and her dog emerging from the mists of the Welsh hills, to a Durham Dales snigger attending to his Dales pony

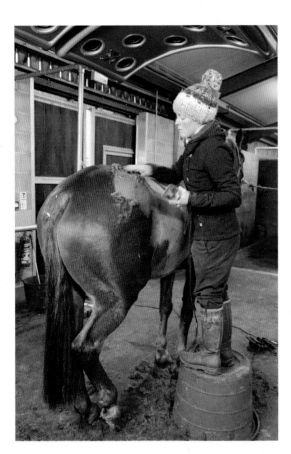

patter of horses' hoofs, creating a memorable snapshot of horsey life. Joyce began showing horses at the age of seven, moving on to set up her business in 1972. 'It's a living' is the answer to a question about commercial efficacy. And why take on the daily burden, the grind of dawn rising come rain or shine? 'Wouldn't give it up whatever' is the answer. Joyce and Jacky do a lot of work with the disabled, something they find particularly rewarding. 'We had a little girl not long ago, and when they sat her on the pony, she couldn't sit up,' Joyce recalls. 'She had to lay down, but she loved touching the horse; her head was on the horse's neck, and they said that just the warmth and the feel of that pony had an effect. Within three or four weeks she was sitting up. They couldn't believe the change in that time. You never see a disabled child miserable on a pony, do you? ... Horses are very forgiving. They don't judge.'

Equine therapy informed other parts of my journey, spirituality surrounding the history of the horse, and the measure of human empathy with the equine. There was Monty Roberts, the American inspiration for 1980s dramas around books, films and documentaries about 'horse whisperers'. There was Jemma Lucas, the soft-spoken, shy horsewoman who is working to be the saviour of the Eriskay pony. Having first come across Monty Roberts in Surrey of all places, he impressed me with his forthright manner, firm beliefs in developing horse sense as an extended expression of human emotion, and the passion of a man with a mission. His life's journey has become a practical crusade to transform equine training techniques shorn of any violence, something which has been (and remains) common in the breaking in of horses. Roberts is not a man who suffers fools easily. Not without his detractors, he is nothing if not straight, as straight as his Cherokee ancestors' arrows. 'There's a lot of very, very violent enemies out there that don't want me around at all,' he whispers. A survivor of childhood domestic violence, he works with ex-veterans, trauma victims, youth at risk and prisoners with the horse as his therapy animal. 'The horse is all body language, but about 70 per cent of what we say is body language anyway, so [body language in horses and humans is] the same,' he observes.

For Jemma Lucas, the idea that equine therapy is a possible cure for many physical and mental conditions, including trauma, is an unexpected revelation. Lucas has three children, two of whom are autistic. Having gone through the necessary training and with the inner strength of an outwardly shy and retiring personality, Lucas' first priority, after saving the Eriskay pony, is to help children and disabled adults. In the process she's managed one of her teenage sons' recovery from autism.

My own recovery from the challenging process of creating *Equine Journeys* is in some measure spiritual – restitution for the long journey in search of the British horse, a realm of magic travelled over a year of open-minded discovery and adventure. No Paul Revere am I, riding this trail to bring good or bad news. The health and wealth of the horse

industry in Britain is good news without a doubt, while the widening chasms between city and country bode ill for the socio-cultural and political health of British society. The spirit and nobility engendered by the horse since the dawn of civilisation have been a transforming elixir for humanity in general. Reverence for the horse should be memorised in some form or other by all, inculcated perhaps more fully in social education and physical endeavour at every level of society.

The horse has much to teach children and adults even after five-and-a-half millennia. This book is not intended as a teaching tool, though, being more of an experiential journey than your common-or-garden book on horses. Nothing has proven more satisfying than to witness the country's social and cultural map, and to revel in the kaleidoscopic beauty of its physical landscapes.

Horsemanship is instilled at a very young age in all classes of British society. (above) Lilly Elizabeth (six) rides her Shetland pony out for a hack accompanied by Hayden Prince (seventeen) at Ford Farm Stables in Brockenhurst, Hampshire

Britannia's Horses

A brief anecdotal history of the horse & the British

Christopher Joll

'Wherever man has left his footprint in the long ascent from barbarism to civilisation, we find the hoof print of a horse beside it.'
— John Trotwood Moore (1858–1929),
   journalist, writer, historian

There is a British Army story that, in the 1890s, a cavalry regiment was formed up on the parade square of its barracks in India, prior to embarking on a train for Bombay, where the men and horses were to be loaded onto a troop ship for the return voyage to England. One horse, however, was missing from the parade: an elderly charger who had come out to India as a young regimental remount twenty years previously but, it was felt, would not survive the long sea voyage home. The adjutant had just called the parade to attention when, from the stables, there was the sound of breaking wood. Moments later, the old horse appeared at a canter and, without a moment's hesitation, took his customary place with his troop. The elderly charger's obvious wish to remain with his regiment was, of course, respected, and the horse duly travelled back to England with his human and equine comrades. Extraordinary as this story may sound, it illustrates the bond of loyalty which for more than two thousand years has bound horses and the British together. What follows is a brief account of that relationship.

Horse domestication & breeding

Evidence from ancient British burial sites indicates that horses were domesticated in Britain from about 2,000 BC, and that by 500 BC they were being ridden and used for pulling war chariots and domestic vehicles. Prior to their domestication, horses were hunted for their meat; it is indicative of the British love of the horse that its meat has not only been absent from British menus for centuries but that its unlabelled presence in prepared foods was at the centre of a food scandal in recent years.

The Uffington White Horse in Oxfordshire is a 360-foot-long chalk carving that probably dates from the period during which horses were domesticated. Its precise symbolism is unclear, although it may be religious given that horses were part of Anglo-Saxon paganism and that the carving is aligned with the midwinter sun. During World War II, the carving was turfed over to prevent it being used by German bombers as a navigational point. The tradition of scrubbing the chalk every seven years – to prevent the carving disappearing – was a local community ritual until the late nineteenth century; it has been restored by the White Horse's current owner, the National Trust, albeit without the traditional, semi-pagan ceremony.

The selective breeding of horses and the importation into Britain of new bloodlines started in the reign of King John, who is best remembered for losing the Crown Jewels in The Wash. He imported a hundred stallions from Flanders with a view to improving the quality of horses bred for the tournament lists. King Edward III, a keen racing man, imported fifty stallions from Spain as they were noted for their speed. King Henry VIII, when not divorcing or beheading his wives, appointed a Master of the Posts in 1516 to improve horse-borne mail delivery. He also introduced legislation to control the breeding and export of horses: the Breed of Horses Act of 1535 and the Horses Act of 1540, both of which are still on the UK's statute books.

Prior to the English Civil War of the mid-seventeenth century, which arose out of a tussle for power between King and Parliament, King Charles I, another monarch with a passion for racing and hunting, focused horse breeding on those two sports to the detriment of the heavier, slower horses required for the Army. This was reversed by Lord Protector Oliver Cromwell, a spoilsport of a man who, having deposed and then decapitated Charles I, banned racing and concentrated on the breeding of cavalry horses.

(below) Aerial view of the Uffington White Horse, an Iron Age chalk figure carved into the hills of Oxfordshire. © National Trust Images

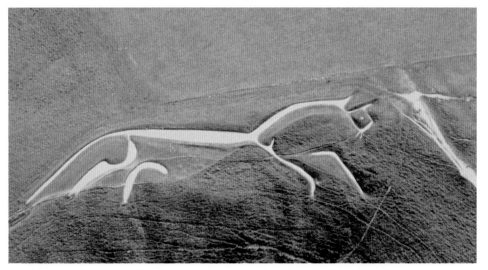

After the Restoration of the Monarchy in 1660, the much jollier reign of King Charles II saw the resumption of breeding horses for racing, a sport much helped by royal patronage. Most importantly in the history of British horse breeding, however, towards the end of the Merry Monarch's reign and during that of Queen Anne – herself a royal 'brood mare' who had seventeen pregnancies but no surviving children (resulting in the end of the rule of the Stuarts) – the thoroughbred bloodline was developed for racing with the import of Arab, Barb and Turk horses for cross-breeding with native English horses.

The Darley Arabian – foaled in 1700 in Aleppo, Syria, at the camp of the Bedouin Sheikh Mirza II – was originally named Ras el Fedowi (The Headstrong One), Manak or Manica; it is unclear which. As a mature horse, he stood at only 15 hands; this was considered at the time to be tall for a Muniqui Arabian. In 1702, he was bought for the very large sum of 300 guineas (2018: £60,000) by Thomas Darley, His Majesty's Consul in the Levant. However, before the horse could be shipped home, Sheikh Mirza reneged on the deal, and Darley had to smuggle the horse out of Syria with the assistance of some British sailors. The Darley Arabian arrived at his new owner's family's stud at Aldby Park in Yorkshire in 1704. Although the horse never raced, between 1705 and 1719 he covered many mares, most of whose progeny were characterised by great speed and stamina. By 1722, he was Britain's leading stud stallion and had sired the undefeated Flying Childers; his great-grandson was the legendary, also undefeated, Eclipse. The Darley Arabian is now considered to be the most important of the three founding sires of the English thoroughbred, with 95 per cent of today's thoroughbreds carrying a Y-chromosome gene that can be traced back to him.

In modern times, many traditional English breeds have come under threat, particularly heavy horses and some ponies, and there are currently initiatives to save such bloodlines as the Cleveland Bay, the Eriskay pony, the Hackney horse and pony, and the Suffolk horse.

The horse & the economy

While Britain's monarchs were encouraging the development of breeds for specialist purposes, horses of all colours were an integral and developing part of the country's economy. From the Iron Age to the end of the Middle Ages, they were primarily used for the transport of goods and people, but by the Tudor period of the fifteenth century horses were being used in farming in place of oxen. It was the development of the horse-drawn plough in the Stuart period that saw the horse become the single most important asset for farmers in Britain's then predominantly agrarian economy. The following observation by Jean Froissart, an author and court historian from the Low Countries, was made about human beings, but it applies almost equally to the horse's role in British agriculture: '[They] are bound by law and custom to plough the fields of their masters, harvest the corn, gather it into barns, and thresh and winnow the grain; they must also mow and carry home the hay, cut and collect wood, and perform all manner of tasks of this kind.' This was all to change with the coming of the Industrial Revolution from the mid-eighteenth to the mid-nineteenth century, during which time, until the widespread adoption of the steam engine, horsepower was a critical component in industry, on the canals, in the mines, and for road communications including mail coaches and horse-drawn omnibuses.

On the London road at Winterslow near Salisbury in Wiltshire is a public house called The Pheasant. During World War II, it was commandeered as an officers' mess by the nearby RAF station at Middle Wallop for the Battle of Britain pilots stationed there. These pilots, who were some of Churchill's famous 'few' (including the author's father), when not repulsing the Germans' air attacks, chalked their names on a board that is still *in situ* behind the bar. More than 120 years before the Battle of Britain, on the night of 20 October 1816, customers of the same pub had come under attack from an equally ferocious foe – a lion that had escaped from Ballard's travelling menagerie then camped on Salisbury Plain. After the lion's Houdini-like escape from its cage, the hungry beast had stalked Quicksilver, the Exeter-to-London mail coach, until, just outside The Pheasant, it pounced on Pomegranate, the coach's off-lead horse. The terrified driver and his passengers rushed into the pub and locked themselves in, leaving the guard, Joseph Pike (who fortunately was armed with a blunderbuss), and Pomegranate to their fate. However, before Pike could shoot the valuable lion, its owner appeared, and his pet Newfoundland dog chased off the big cat, which was later caught. Sadly, the Newfoundland dog was killed in the chase, but, happily for horse lovers, Pomegranate survived. Although attacks on mail coaches by wild animals were extremely rare, other travellers at other times faced the ever-present danger of highwaymen, footpads and – in winter – the mud, a notorious feature of Britain's largely unpaved roads, into which whole coaching teams were reported to have to disappeared.

(above) Ploughing with a wheeled plough drawn by two horses and led by a ploughboy. Woodcut from *Great Inventors*, London, c. 1882. Courtesy of The World History Archive

(above) Horse-drawn traffic outside the Bank of England in the City of London, 1897. Courtesy of British Pathé

Until the development of the railway system, and given the appalling state of the roads, canals were the motorways of the Industrial Revolution, linking Britain's main manufacturing centres and ports with a network of purpose-built waterways as sophisticated as today's M-roads. The freight barges carrying finished goods, coal, iron and other raw materials were pulled by horses along a towpath.

Despite the canal system, horse-drawn traffic congestion in Britain's cities was every bit as bad, if not worse, in the nineteenth century as it was after the internal combustion engine replaced horsepower in the early twentieth. Pollution was equally bad, with hundreds of tons of horse droppings landing on city streets every day. In London, the problem was so severe that crossing sweepers, usually boys and young men drawn from the poorest of the urban poor, would – much in the same way as today's freelance car-window cleaners – clear away the dung for pedestrians at major intersections for a small tip. Such crossing sweepers were immortalised by Charles Dickens in his mid-Victorian novel *Bleak House*.

The central role of horses in the British economy was eventually phased out from the end of the nineteenth century following the introduction of steam engines in agriculture and industry, and by the internal combustion engine in transport and communications. However, horses continued to be used in some fields of transport, agriculture and the mines until after World War II, and are today still used to pull brewers' drays, royal carriages and the Lord Mayor of London's State Coach.

The war horse

By the time of the Roman invasion of Britain in 55 BC, the Celtic tribes of Britain had developed fleets of war chariots and used horses not as cavalry but rather as a means of moving foot soldiers swiftly on the battlefield. The iconic equestrian statue of Queen Boudicca of the Iceni, sculpted by Thomas Thorneycroft, which stands at the northern end of Westminster Bridge in London, is a highly romanticised image of the warrior Queen, who led an uprising in AD 60 against the Romans after she was flogged and her daughters had been raped. Equally inaccurate are her chariot and the horses pulling it; almost certainly both of these elements would have been considerably more primitive than they are portrayed. During her campaign, Boudicca slaughtered eighty thousand Romans; she was eventually defeated at the Battle of Watling Street in AD 61 and shortly thereafter either committed suicide or died of disease.

In the Anglo-Saxon era, mounted soldiers were an important military resource on the battlefield, and it is probable that King Harold II lost the Battle of Hastings in 1066 to the Norman invader, King William I, because his horsed troops were still in the north of England. King Harold's lack of cavalry is graphically illustrated in the Bayeux Tapestry, sewn within a few years of the battle, possibly by Queen Matilda, the wife of King William I, and her ladies.

During the Middle Ages, the concept of cavalry as shock troops on the battlefield was starting to develop,

(right) Noblemen jousting. Illustration from an Augsburg manuscript by Paulus Héctor Mair, c. 1540. Courtesy of the Bavarian State Library

(above) A Parliamentarian Trooper fires his carbine at Powick Bridge, the first major cavalry engagement of the English Civil War. Gouache by Graham Turner from *Ironsides*, 2002. © Osprey Publishing

aided by a deliberate attempt at improvements in equine size, strength and agility, encouraged through knightly tournaments and jousting, which were romanticised in verse by Chaucer, Shakespeare and others. Jousting started in the early Middle Ages as training for warfare; it quickly developed into a stylised but dangerous competitive leisure activity – with heavily romantic overtones – for knights, aristocrats and monarchs. By the end of the sixteenth century in Britain, jousting had become a largely ceremonial affair. It was discontinued altogether shortly after the marriage celebrations of King Charles I, only to be revived in recent years as an exciting display at county shows and medieval re-enactments. The development of cavalry tactics advanced considerably during the English Civil War, in which Cromwell's new so-called 'Ironsides' were as decisive in some of the later battles as the tank would be at the end of World War I. The armour worn by the Ironsides, consisting of a breast- and back-plate and a metal helmet, was clearly derived from medieval full-body armour but was considerably reduced in body coverage and weight. This allowed the Ironsides to ride faster horses than their medieval predecessors. This type of heavy cavalry horse is still in use by the Household Cavalry, who also wear armour not dissimilar to that worn by Cromwell's cavalry.

The role of cavalry in warfare reached its apotheosis during the Napoleonic Wars with more than thirty thousand horses engaged at the Battle of Waterloo (1815), 50 per cent of whom were killed or had to be destroyed later. To give some idea of the scale of the cavalry presence at Waterloo, if all the horses on the battlefield had been lined up, knee-to-knee, in a single rank, the line would have stretched for more than 17 miles. At Waterloo, the Allied commander, Field Marshal the Duke of Wellington, rode a dark chestnut thoroughbred-cross-Arab stallion called Copenhagen. The horse, who stood 15 hands, had been foaled in 1808 and was initially used as a flat racehorse, winning two races and finishing 'in the frame' in all but one of his twelve races. Copenhagen was acquired by Wellington in 1813 and quickly became his favourite charger. On the day of the battle, the Field Marshal was on this horse continuously for seventeen hours. When the victorious Allied commander at last dismounted, he gave Copenhagen a friendly pat on the rump; without warning, the stallion lashed out with its near rear leg, missing Wellington's head by a couple of inches. Despite this, the Duke continued to ride the horse on parade, eventually retiring him to his country house, Stratfield Saye, where Copenhagen grazed away his days until his death in 1836, thereby outliving the Duke's great enemy, Emperor Napoleon I, by fifteen years and the Emperor's horse at Waterloo, Marengo, by five. Unlike Marengo, whose skeleton is on display at the National Army Museum and whose front hooves were made into silver-mounted snuff mills, Copenhagen was buried at Stratfield Saye, where – minus a front hoof, which was, to the fury of the Duke, illicitly removed before the interment – he lies beneath an inscribed headstone. The missing hoof was eventually returned to the Wellington family, and the 2nd Duke had it made into a silver mounted inkwell.

In the nineteenth century, the ill-fated Charge of the Light Brigade at the Battle of Balaclava (1854) during the Crimean War came to symbolise the ineptness of the Anglo-French high command while at the same time romanticising the British cavalry. The lesser-known Charge of the Heavy Brigade, which preceded that of the Lights, was in fact a successful operation very much against the odds: the British cavalry was inferior in numbers to their Russian opponents, whom (contrary to accepted practice) they charged uphill and routed despite the British sabres being unable to penetrate the Russian cavalry's heavy overcoats.

Although without the posthumous fame of Wellington's Copenhagen, the Earl of Cardigan's chestnut thoroughbred charger, Ronald, which he rode at the head of the Light Brigade, was somewhat gruesomely memorialised. Ronald outlived his master and had a starring role at his funeral in 1868, but when the horse died – unlike Copenhagen – his head was stuffed, his tail preserved, and all four of his hooves were made into elaborate silver-gilt inkwells, while the remainder of his carcass was sent to the local hunt's kennels. The chestnut's preserved head, tail and one of the hoof inkwells are still on display at Lord Cardigan's country seat, Deene Park; a second hoof inkwell was given to Cardigan's regiment, the 11th Hussars, and can be seen at the King's Royal Hussars Museum in Winchester. The third hoof, which was presented to King Edward VII, is on display in the Royal Collection at Windsor Castle, while the last hoof was given to a family friend and has disappeared from public view altogether.

Until relatively recently, the British Army has often recruited to its cavalry regiments those officers with a closer association to the hunting field than the library. Between 1850 and 1899, the two regiments of Life Guards included seventy-seven members of the landed aristocracy, the Royal Horse Guards boasted a further thirty-nine, and the ultra-fashionable 10th Hussars had the Heir Presumptive, HRH Prince Albert Victor, Duke of Clarence and Avondale, as a serving officer. It is a fact that, prior to 1947, only those gentlemen cadets entering the Royal Military College, Sandhurst with top academic grades qualified for the infantry. Winston Churchill's father, Lord Randolph Churchill, was particularly irritated with his son when, with dismal academic results, he only qualified to join the 4th Hussars rather that the King's Royal Rifle Corps for which his father had destined him.

The view of the British cavalry as a gorgeously uniformed if somewhat redundant appendage to the rest of the Army was widespread in the late Victorian forces partly because there were no colonial wars or campaigns in which cavalry could be fully deployed. This situation changed in 1882, when a nationalist revolt in Egypt had to be supressed by a conventional British Expeditionary Force consisting of cavalry, infantry and artillery. This short campaign included the famous and successful moonlight charge at Kassassin

(below) *The Duke of Wellington at Waterloo*. Oil on canvas by Robert Alexander Hillingford, 1800s. © Christie's Images/ Bridgeman Images

(above) *Charge of the 9th Lancers to save the guns at Mons.* by Archibald Webb, © UIG History/Science & Society Picture Library

by the Household Cavalry, who had not been operationally deployed for sixty-seven years since the Battle of Waterloo.

By the start of the twentieth century, the role of horsed cavalry in set-piece warfare was in decline, although it was still to have its moments of glory. In 1898, General Sir Herbert Kitchener led an Anglo-Egyptian Expeditionary Force to retake the Sudan from the insurgent Mahdists. Included under his command was a single British cavalry regiment, the 21st Lancers (Empress of India's). In the advance to Omdurman following the successful battle of the same name, Kitchener ordered the Lancers – in accordance with their conventional role – to reconnoitre and clear the country between his main force and the enemy-held city. In the course of this task, they came under fire from a few hundred Mahdists in the open. Attached to the 21st Lancers, in search of fame and glory but against Kitchener's express wishes, was young Lieutenant Winston Churchill of the 4th Hussars.

As the result of an earlier accident in which he had dislocated his right shoulder, which remained loose in its socket, Churchill wisely decided against using a sword in action and instead had armed himself with a Mauser automatic pistol. No sooner were the enemy's shots whistling over their heads than the Lancers' commanding officer ordered his bugler to sound the calls that would bring the four hundred men of the 21st Lancers, armed (except for Churchill) with lances and swords, from column into line and then from the walk to the trot and, finally, to

the charge. Unbeknownst to them, behind the Dervishes in the open was an enemy force of twenty-five hundred troops concealed in a *nullah*, or dry watercourse. In the ensuing action, the Lancers sustained seventy men killed or wounded, lost 119 horses and earned three Victoria Crosses. It was the last cavalry charge by a regimental formation in British history.

During the Second Boer War at the turn of the twentieth century, which started with a series of besieged British garrisons but developed into a war of movement, the British Army deployed thousands of cavalrymen. However, because of the unconventional nature of the combat, they were armed with rifles rather than with lances and swords. Initially, the British cavalry used horses shipped from England, but, by the end of the war, the Army had lost to disease, exhaustion and combat more than four hundred thousand horses, two-thirds of which were imported from Australia, whose hardy bush ponies were better suited to the South African terrain than native-born British cavalry horses. The Household Cavalry Composite Regiment started the Boer War with 550 horses; by the time peace was declared in 1902, they had lost a staggering 3,275.

At the 1902 Royal Tournament, the salute was taken at one of the performances by Queen Alexandra, who was briefed that the lead horse of the 2nd Life Guards Quadrille, Freddy (D36), had not only served in the Second Boer War but was the only 2nd Life Guard horse to have survived the regiment's deployment in South Africa. Queen Alexandra noticed that Freddy was not wearing a campaign medal and enquired why. No-one knew the answer. A brisk exchange of letters between Buckingham Palace and the War Office followed. At first, the Commander-in-Chief, Field Marshal the 1st Earl Roberts of Kandahar VC, was adamant: military animals did *not* receive campaign medals, although – hypocritically – his own horse, Volonel, had been awarded by Queen Victoria the Afghan Medal with four clasps, the Afghan Star and the 1897 Jubilee Medal. The Queen was unimpressed by this reply and continued to lobby on behalf of Freddy. Nine months later, the War Office hauled up a white flag, and Freddy was awarded a Boer War medal with five clasps bearing the words *Wittenberg, Kimberley, Paarderberg, Driefontein* and *Transvaal*. The medal was stitched onto the breastplate of his horse furniture, and, until he was retired in 1905, he wore it on every parade and duty. Freddy passed his retirement at Combermere Barracks, Windsor, dying there in 1911. His body was buried beneath the barracks' square, and his medal was eventually placed on display in the Household Cavalry Museum, London.

In the early stages of World War I in Europe and in the closing stages of that war in the Middle East, the British Army deployed horsed cavalry in significant numbers. In Belgium and France, in August and September 1914, the British 1st Cavalry Division consisting of ten thousand horses covered the retreat from Mons and suffered heavy casualties. The 9th Queen's Royal Lancers had been sent to France in August 1914 as part of the 1st Cavalry Division; Captain Francis Grenfell of the 9th was awarded the Victoria Cross for his actions in saving the guns of 119th Battery, Royal Field Artillery, on 24 August 1914. Only a month later, the regiment had the distinction of engaging in the final cavalry-against-cavalry action on the Western Front, when, on 7 September 1914 at Montcel à Frétoy, Lieutenant Colonel David Campbell led a charge of two troops of his Lancers against a squadron of the Prussian Dragoons of the Guard and routed them. By the end of the year, a second cavalry division had been formed, but by then trenches had been dug by both sides and the war had settled into one of static and bloody attrition. Nonetheless, in the hope that there would be a breakthrough of the German lines which could be exploited by mounted soldiers, the British cavalry was kept in reserve. In due course, its men were also required to fight in the trenches as infantry.

Meanwhile, in the Middle East, from the middle of 1916, the Turkish lines of communication were increasingly disrupted by Arab-horsed and camel-borne irregulars led by Major T. E. Lawrence, better known as Lawrence of Arabia, and the Turkish garrisons in Arabia were progressively besieged by the Arab Army commanded by Prince Faisal, later King Faisal I of Iraq. This allowed the

(below) *The 21st Lancers at Omdurman, Sudan.* Oil on canvas by William Barns Wollen, 1899. Courtesy of the Cavalry and Guards Club and Defence Academy of the United Kingdom

(above) Rehearsal for
HM The Queen's birthday
parade, 3 June 2012.
Courtesy of Richard
Symonds

Egyptian Expeditionary Force, under the command of a
cavalry soldier, General Sir Edmund Allenby, to initiate
a successful offensive in 1917 against the Turko-German
Armies in the Levant. In the fast-moving campaign which
followed, Allenby employed the 4th Cavalry Division,
comprising Indian Army cavalry and British yeomanry
regiments, in his march on Jerusalem and Damascus. After
the end of the war in the Middle East, the division remained
in Palestine until 1921, when its yeomanry regiments
returned to Britain and their horses were sold to local
farmers and businesses. The pitiful condition into which
these animals fell was noticed some years later by Dorothy
Brooke, the wife of a senior British cavalry officer in Cairo.
Following the publication of a letter she wrote to the *Daily
Telegraph* about the condition of these ex-British war horses,
donations flooded in. Using these resources, Mrs Brooke
established The Brooke Charity to provide veterinary
hospitals and, later, education for the owners
of horses and mules in emerging markets as to how best
to treat their animals.

The deployment of mounted troops on the battlefield
was only phased out by the British Army in 1941 after the
1st Cavalry Division's horses in Palestine were exchanged
for trucks. Nonetheless, after World War II, horses were
re-introduced for state ceremonial duties by the Household
Cavalry and the King's Troop Royal Horse Artillery. That
does not mean, however, that horses have been out of
Britain's front line with domestic terrorism. This was

tragically the case when, on 20 July 1982, the Provisional
Irish Republican Army (PIRA) detonated a large bomb
packed with nails in a parked car on the South Carriage
Drive in London's Hyde Park. The bomb was triggered at
exactly the moment that the Queen's Life Guard was riding
by on its way to Horse Guards for the daily Guard Mounting
Ceremony. An officer, a warrant officer, a lance corporal
and a trooper of the Blues and Royals were killed along with
seven of their black horses.

The worst injured of the cavalry 'blacks' to survive
the PIRA bomb, after eight hours of surgery, was a Blues
and Royals charger called Sefton who became a national
hero, was made Horse of the Year 1982 and was placed in
the British Horse Society's Hall of Fame. Foaled in Ireland
in 1963, Sefton for a time served as a remount with the
Household Cavalry in Germany, where his prodigious
jumping skills put him much in demand as a hunter. Sefton
was not, however, an easy horse: he only liked certain riders
(including the author) and would buck off those that he
did not like; he would only be hunted in a snaffle bit, with
the reins held 'on the buckle' by his rider; and, once a day,
when hunting with the Household Cavalry's Weser Vale
Bloodhounds, he would choose a fence – large or small,
the size did not seem to matter – at which to refuse. After
his recovery from the PIRA bomb, Sefton served with the
Blues and Royals in London for another three years. He was
retired in 1984 and put down, aged thirty, in 1993 due to
incurable lameness arising from his bomb injuries.

The horse, Society & sport

The possession of an elegant, handsome or outstanding horse has always conferred prestige on its owner. In Georgian times, rich young aristocrats, known as Corinthians, paid huge sums and took great risks to race specially built carriages pulled by matched teams of horses – equipages that were the equivalent of today's Ferraris and Porsches. These nail-biting races were immortalised by Sir Arthur Conan Doyle in his 1896 novel about Regency 'bucks', dandies and Corinthians, *Rodney Stone*.

In the nineteenth century, London Society, which was considerably more sedate but no less licentious than its Regency incarnation, would parade on Rotten Row every afternoon during the Season (Easter to late June) on beautifully groomed horses and in exquisite horse-drawn carriages. When not showing off in Rotten Row, London Society could be found at the races. The fashion for the 'Sport of Kings' started after the Restoration and reached its apogee in the Edwardian era with must-attend race meetings at Ascot, Newmarket, Epsom and Doncaster.

In the twentieth century, the sport was twice blighted by politics. First, in 1913, when a Suffragette, Emily Davison, threw herself under the King's horse, Anmer, at the Derby and was killed. Then, in 1983, the Derby winner, Shergar, was kidnapped for ransom by the Provisional IRA and never seen again. On a happier note, racing also created heroes, most notably Foinavon, the winner of the 1967 Grand National. The horse was the 100–1 outsider for the race, and for the first circuit and a half of the Aintree course was at the back of the field. Then, at the twenty-third fence, there was a massive pile-up which, because he was so far back, Foinavon managed to avoid. With the course clear in front of him, he led the remaining field over the last six jumps to win the race. Subsequently, a fence was named after the winning horse at Aintree.

The equally fashionable sport of polo had been introduced to Britain in 1869 by the ultra-exclusive 10th Hussars and quickly became the sport of princes and cavalry officers, who still play the game today. When not playing polo, cavalry regiments and the Royal Horse Artillery organised musical quadrilles – synchronised horse drills performed to live music – which were a popular part of county shows and the annual Royal Tournament. The Musical Drive of the King's Troop Royal Horse Artillery and the Musical Ride of the Household Cavalry are still performed today.

During the winter, nineteenth-century London Society retired to the country for hunting and, when the hunting season closed, for point-to-pointing. These horsed activities attracted all classes, from tenant farmers to royalty, while their children had fun on their ponies at gymkhanas and in competitions organised by the Pony Club. In the twentieth century, sports derived from hunting and gymkhanas – most notably three-day eventing, show jumping and dressage – became popular with the public, and the UK's ongoing success in international competitions, and at the Olympic Games, made stars of horses such as Foxhunter and, most recently, Valegro.

(above) *A Gentleman with His Pair of Bays Harnessed to a Curricle*. Oil on canvas by John Cordrey, 1806. Courtesy of the Yale Center for British Art, Paul Mellon Collection, New Haven

(above) *A Game of Polo*. Hand-coloured engraving by James E. Kelly from *Harper's Weekly*, 1882. Courtesy of Prints Old & Rare, Pacifica, California

(left) *'Paddy', Drummer of His Majesty's 1st Life Guards*. Painting by Sir Alfred Munnings, 1922. Courtesy of Household Cavalry Museum. (opposite) *Whistlejacket*. Oil on canvas by George Stubbs, 1762. Courtesy of The National Gallery, London

The horse & the arts

Given the importance of the horse in every aspect of British culture, it is not surprising that famous horses – both real and imaginary – should have been immortalised in painting, sculpture, literature, poetry, folk songs, plays and film. Two of Britain's greatest artists were celebrated horse painters: George Stubbs and Sir Alfred Munnings.

The portrait of Whistlejacket by Stubbs is generally acknowledged as artistically revolutionary in its life-size depiction of the Marquess of Rockingham's racehorse against a plain background. For generations, it hung in the Whistlejacket Room at Wentworth Woodhouse, the Yorkshire country seat of the Fitzwilliam family – a house with the longest façade and the coldest rooms in England. In 1997, the painting was acquired by the National Gallery,

London, for £11 million. The half life-size painting of Paddy, the Drum Horse of the 1st Life Guards, was painted by Munnings in 1922 for Colonel Sir George Holford, Bt, who had acquired the horse for his regiment and who then gave the painting to his fellow officers. Students of equine military history will note that Paddy is depicted with 'clean heels' whereas today's Household Cavalry Drum Horses retain their fetlock 'feathers'. In the field of literature, *Black Beauty* by Anna Sewell (1820–1878) is one of Britain's best-loved children's stories, while *Gulliver's Travels* by the satirist Jonathan Swift (1667–1745) features a nation ruled by wise talking horses who have no word for lying, and Sir Michael Morpurgo's *War Horse* was made into a hit stage play and a film directed by the legendary Steven Spielberg.

BY ROYAL AUTHORITY.

A New Way of mounting your Horse in spite of the GOUT!! *Dedicated to all fashionable Equestrians afflicted with that Malady!*—

(above) The gouty Prince Regent being helped onto his horse by means of an elaborate contraption outside an oriental pavilion in Kew Gardens. Coloured etching printed by J. Sidebotham, London, 1816. Courtesy of the Wellcome Collection

The horse & royalty

Throughout the ages, horses and royalty have been inseparable. Shakespeare has King Richard III desperately calling for a horse at the Battle of Bosworth Field in 1485; Queen Elizabeth I famously rode a white palfry in full armour to rally her troops at Tilbury before the Spanish Armada in 1588; King Charles I, who was a very short man, appears lofty and regal in Van Dyck's famous equestrian portrait of him; while in exile, King Charles II 'invented' the Household Cavalry; Jacobites celebrated the death of King William III with a toast to the 'gentleman in the little black velvet waistcoat', a reference to the mole hole that caused the King's fall from his horse and subsequent death; and King George II, who to the dismay of his generals took command of his troops at the Battle of Dettingen in 1743, had to relinquish command when his horse bolted with him.

King George III, who is now best known for the mental disorder which blighted the second half of his reign, was particularly fond of the Royal Horse Guards (the Blues), so much so that he bought for the regiment the land on which is now situated Combermere Barracks, the home headquarters of the Household Cavalry. In further displays of royal affection for the regiment, George III adapted the Blues' distinctive blue tunic with red collars and cuffs as the royal family's and royal household's uniform when in residence at Windsor Castle, an order of dress which is still worn today. He also gave the regiment a massive pair of silver kettle drums, which were so heavy that the regiment had to acquire a Shire horse to carry them. Finally, he appointed himself a captain in the regiment, in which capacity he would turn up at parades unannounced and, when the commanding officer ordered a Royal Salute, the King would shout, 'No, no, Colonel – I am just Captain King.'

As a young man, King George IV was a keen horseman who is depicted in the saddle in several bronze statues and many portraits, most notably in a painting by George Stubbs. In later life, as Prince Regent and then as King, George became so fat and so afflicted with gout that he could not climb stairs. On the rare occasions when he appeared mounted, he had to be winched into the saddle of a sturdy 'heavy' horse like a medieval knight. As the *Times* reported on 25 March 1816, when the Prince Regent appeared on parade in the uniform of a Field Marshal and sporting the Waterloo medal (to which he was not entitled), 'An inclined plane was constructed ... at the upper end of which was a platform. His Royal Highness was placed in a chair on rollers, and so moved up the ascent, and placed on the platform, which was then raised by screws, high enough to pass the horse under: and finally, His Royal Highness was gently let down into the saddle.' The event was subsequently, if perhaps a little inaccurately, lampooned in a cartoon by George Cruickshank. King George IV detested his father, King George III, but nonetheless immortalised him – almost certainly ironically – with a giant bronze equestrian statue bearing a Latin inscription that translates as 'The Best of Fathers'. Known as The Copper Horse, it was sculpted by Sir

Richard Westmacott and erected after George IV's death on rising ground at the end of the Long Walk in Windsor Great Park in 1831. It is so large that, inside the belly (accessed by a trap door) are a table and chairs that are used when the sculpture is periodically cleaned.

Like her uncle, Queen Victoria was an energetic horsewoman, but by middle age and following the birth of nine children, she had become too stout to ride anything much friskier than a led Highland pony. In the last years of her reign, the nearest that she got to a horse was driving a small pony-drawn gig or riding in a carriage. For her Diamond Jubilee Parade of 1897, the Queen was driven in an open semi-state landau pulled by eight Hanoverian Creams from Buckingham Palace to St Paul's Cathedral, where an outdoor service of thanksgiving was held, and then back to the palace via the South Bank. The route, which was 6 miles long, was lined all the way by shoulder-to-shoulder uniformed soldiers and sailors. The royal procession consisted of seventeen carriages, dozens of the Queen's royal relations from across Europe and assorted royal rulers from within the Empire, all mounted, and eight thousand cavalry of the Empire. It was probably the largest number of horses ever to appear as one formation on London's streets. The sovereign's escort on this occasion was furnished by the 2nd Life Guards, whose commanding

(above) Queen Victoria, with Princess Victoria of Schleswig-Holstein, in a carriage on the lawn of Osborne House, 1892. Courtesy of Mary Evans/The National Archives, London

(right) Colonel of the 10th Hussars, HRH The Prince of Wales (George Frederick Ernest Albert, later King George V), c. 1800. Courtesy of Universal History Archive/Getty Images

officer, the Earl of Dundonald, rode just behind the Queen's carriage. Having trouble with his mare, he repeatedly tried to calm her by saying, 'Steady, old lady! Whoa, old girl!' For the early part of the procession, Queen Victoria thought that he was talking to her. Lord Macdonald was luckier than Lord Howe, the elderly colonel of the 2nd Life Guards, who in his heavy uniform topped with a helmet and cuirasses was overcome by the heat, fainted and fell off his horse.

King Edward VII, whose portly figure was not well suited to riding, is best known to equine posterity for his love of the turf and his patronage of both flat and National Hunt racing. Initially his horses were trained by John Porter at Kingsclear, who persuaded the Prince of Wales, as he then was, to buy Perdita II. From this mare were bred Persimmon, the winner of the 1896 Derby and the 1897 Ascot Gold Cup; and Diamond Jubilee, who in 1900 won the 2,000 Guineas, the Derby and the St Leger. Both horses were trained by Richard Marsh, who was the royal trainer from 1892. Between 1900 and 1909, there was a decline in Edward's racing luck, until he leased Minoru from Colonel William Hall-Walker (later Lord Wavertree). Minoru won the 2,000 Guineas and the Derby in 1909, a year before the King's death. The only British sovereign to have won the Derby three times, King Edward VII's reign ended on 6 May 1910. Appropriately for the most successful racehorse-owning British monarch, shortly before he died the King was informed by the about-to-be King George V that his horse Witch of the Air had won the 4.15 p.m. race at Kempton Park. 'I am so glad,' said the dying King. They were the last words that he spoke.

King George V, who invented the modern British monarchy, despite his upbringing as a sailor understood the importance of the horse as part of royal imagery.

It was for this reason that, in October 1915, he was mounted when he reviewed troops marching to the Western Front. The cheering of the men unsettled the King's horse, which, without warning, reared up, threw the King from the saddle and then rolled on top of him. Fortunately, the ground was soft, otherwise the King would have been crushed to death. As it was, he was severely bruised and never fully recovered from the accident. After World War I, George V's eldest son, the future King Edward VIII, who did not have a very firm seat on a horse, took to polo, hunting and steeplechasing with a great deal more enthusiasm than skill. His frequent falls were widely reported in the press, which caused the King concern, not because he was worried that the heir to the throne would break his neck – after all, he had three healthy younger brothers – but because he believed the Prince's lack of riding skills would be a problem for him with the British public, who admired a good seat on a horse.

In a desperate attempt to correct this fault, the King engaged a White Russian ex-cavalry Colonel and former equerry to the Tsar of Russia, Count Paul Rodzianko, to give the Prince of Wales riding lessons. Rodzianko, who would go on to train the Irish show-jumping team, is principally known to posterity as the man who rescued Joy, the Tsarevitch's spaniel, which had been with the imperial family in the cellar of Ipatiev House when they were murdered but had escaped the slaughter. After six frustrating weeks in the indoor riding school at the Royal Mews, Rodzianko stormed into George V's study, thumped the royal desk and shouted at the King, 'My dear, good, blasted Majesty, your son is no bloody good!' This was an opinion which, in 1936, was to be shared by the rest of the nation – albeit for different reasons – when Edward VIII abdicated in order to marry the twice-divorced American socialite Wallis Simpson.

(left) HM King George V inspecting troops of the 9th Division at Dunchurch, near Leamington, prior to their departure for Gallipoli, 1915. © Imperial War Museum

(above) HM The Queen at the Trooping of the Colour in London, 1976. Courtesy of Trinity Mirror/Mirrorpix/ Alamy Stock Photo

Today's British royal family are even more distinguished than their forebears by their love of the horse and their skills in the saddle. HM The Queen owns a string of racehorses and a stud and is still riding at the age of ninety-three. When she was shot at on The Mall in 1981 while riding her horse, Burmese, to the Queen's Birthday Parade (Trooping the Colour), her first concern was for her horse. HRH The Duke of Edinburgh was an accomplished polo player until he had to abandon the game in favour of the more sedentary, but highly competitive, carriage driving, a sport which he still pursues at the age of ninety-six. HRH The Prince of Wales was also a keen polo player and a follower to hounds, although he had to give up hunting when it was banned in 2004. His sister, The Princess Royal, and her daughter Zara Tindall are both distinguished three-day event competitors at international level. The Princess Royal won two silver medals in the 1975 European Eventing Championships, riding her horse Doublet, and competed in the 1976 Olympic Games on HM The Queen's horse, Goodwill. Zara Tindall has won many medals for eventing including a team silver at the 2012 Olympic Games.

The importance of the horse to the British people is a simple historical fact. Looking ahead, although state ceremonial may be cut back, technology may replace flesh-and-blood, and fashions in sport and leisure may change, the place of the horse in the hearts of the British people continues to fulfil the same role as the words that run through a stick of Brighton rock.

(above) (L–R) Britain's Zara Phillips, Kristina Cook, Mary King, Nicola Wilson and William Fox-Pitt after receiving their silver medals at the Eventing Team Jumping victory ceremony, London 2012 Olympic Games, Greenwich Park, 31 July 2012. Courtesy of REUTERS/Eddie Keogh

(far left) HRH The Duke of Edinburgh competes in the International Driving Grand Prix at the Royal Windsor Horse Show in Berkshire, 2003. Courtesy of Stefan Rousseau/PA Archive/ PA Images

(left) HM The Queen with one of her horses competing in the Highland classes at the Royal Windsor Horse Show, 2011. Courtesy of Steve Parsons/PA Archive/ PA Images

(left) Horses out to pasture in a bucolic summer meadow, evoking the reflective mood of England's green and pleasant landscapes

Newmarket

Newmarket, Suffolk

It was King James I who introduced the sport of racing to the sleepy village of Newmarket in the early seventeenth century. A lover of equestrian pursuits, he recognised the site's potential and built the first grandstand on the heath. Racing flourished during the reign of Charles II, who had a palace built in the town and, from 1669 onwards, moved his entire court to Newmarket twice a year for the racing season. Newmarket became known as the unofficial capital where affairs of state were conducted alongside racing, hawking and cock-fighting. The first organised races led to the founding of The Jockey Club in 1750; its home is the same site as The Jockey Club Rooms. The greats of British equine art were also attracted to Newmarket, among them George Stubbs and Alfred Munnings.

In 2016, Newmarket Racecourses celebrated 350 years of its oldest race, the Town Plate. Today the town is still regarded as the headquarters of British racing; one in three residents are employed in the sport. Newmarket has two courses: the Rowley Mile and the July Course. More than eighty trainers use the grounds, and there are two or three thousand thoroughbreds in training at any one time. Visitors and tourists attract approximately £9.5 million per annum to the local economy.

The 4,500 acres managed by The Jockey Club in Newmarket include training grounds (turf gallops, artificial gallops and purpose-built horse walks/walking grounds), racecourses, the National Stud, and residential and commercial properties. The National Horseracing Museum is located in the Heritage Centre at Palace House. Having undergone a multi-million-pound restoration funded by the Heritage Lottery Fund and charitable donations, Palace House, the accompanying stable yard and the centre itself were opened by HM The Queen in 2016. Another unique and important presence in the town is that of Tattersalls Bloodstock Auctioneers, the world's oldest bloodstock auctioneers, founded in 1766. Tattersalls offers ten thousand thoroughbred horses each year at fifteen sales at either Newmarket or Fairyhouse outside Dublin.

(right) Horses returning to stables in freezing mid-April fog after their early-morning gallops on Warren Hill, part of The Jockey Club's 2,500 acres of grounds available to all Newmarket stables, each of which pays a nominal fee per month to use the well-kept tracks

(left) Horses in a long queue of early-morning riders in groups separated by the liveries of their stables. There are even equestrian 'traffic wardens' to control the gallop rush hour beginning each morning at 7.00 a.m. (opposite) Two riders from trainer Michael Bell's stable in full gallop – horses and riders let loose as they hit the track, having chafed at the bit waiting their turn

The Farrier
Henry Carnall, Newmarket, Suffolk

Farriery, or the shoeing of horses, is an ancient craft. Modern farriers must have knowledge of the anatomy of horses' feet and legs, be able to work alongside vets, manage and handle horses, understand and meet the needs of clients, and successfully run their own businesses. Horseshoes found in ancient graves suggest that the Celts were probably the first people to protect their horses' feet with nailed-on shoes. The practice then spread through Germany, Gaul and Britain. In 1887, a committee was appointed to consider the establishment of a farriers' register and the setting up of practical examinations. Two years later, the Institute of Horse Shoeing was set up, as well as a register of qualified farriers throughout the country. A great deal of work led to the passing of the Farriers (Registration) Act 1975, which was amended in 1977 'to prevent and avoid suffering by cruelty to horses arising from the shoeing of horses by unskilled persons; to promote the training of farriers and shoeing smiths; to provide for the establishment of a Farriers Registration Council to register persons engaged in farriery and to prohibit the shoeing of horses by unqualified persons'.

'Originally I was a CMC operator for JCB,' says apprentice farrier Henry Carnall. 'I then got put onto four days when I was at sixth form. You are supposed to go through a business or an engineering company, and I said, "I'll go with my mum's farrier."' Now twenty years old, Carnall has been an apprentice farrier for about three years. 'I'll be in at 6 o'clock in the morning,' he says, explaining that he works with a farrier in another race yard who assigns him tasks. 'If we've got a quiet day, he'll say, 'Right, go in the forge; I want such-and-such made.' So the other day I came in and made two sets for horses that we used yesterday. They went straight on. James [the senior farrier] doesn't fit any factory-made shoes unless the horse is in training, so all the hot shoeing is done with handmade ... I'm contracted for ten and a half hours a day plus overtime.'

Apprentice farriers must be supported by an Approved Training Farrier (ATF) who is willing to employ them throughout their apprenticeship. They must purchase all tools and chaps themselves. An apprenticeship runs for four years, after which you sit an exam and then go out on your own. Carnall's 'big ambition would probably be to do the same as James ... When you qualify, you get your diploma ... and then you can go on to do your Associate with the Welsh Company of Farriers. After that you can also do a Fellowship with the Welsh Company of Farriers, and then you can do one higher ... My old boss, Simon Curtis, he's a PhD ... As a qualified lad I got offered, before I started the apprenticeship ... work as soon as I qualified, at £200 a day, flat rate. So if I did three days for one bloke and three days for another bloke, I'd take home just shy of £82,000 a year before tax'.

(far left) Henry Carnall, apprentice farrier, on a cigar break outside the traditional workshop near Warren Hill. Carnall, who earns £3.50 per hour working eleven-hour days, is celebrating the windfall he anticipates once he becomes a licenced professional, whereupon he might earn upwards of £80,000 a year. (left) The hard graft of fashioning a horseshoe is as old as recorded history, with hammer and anvil, and (opposite) the fire of the furnace

Seamus O'Gorman

Work rider, Simon Crisford Racing, Kremlin House Stables, Newmarket, Suffolk

Seamus O'Gorman's desire to become a jockey took hold during his time with Pat Flynn, when he rode Virginia Deer, a horse no-one wanted at the sales but who ended up doing quite well. O'Gorman went on to become an apprentice jockey with Ian Balding in the UK. Following his first experience in Dubai in 1994, he joined Godolphin as a work rider for trainer Saeed bin Suroor, staying at the stud for over thirty years and riding more than two hundred winners. O'Gorman's current boss Simon Crisford (the former Godolphin racing manager) says of him, 'He has gone through the full spectrum of a rider's career from making the transition from apprentice to successful jockey

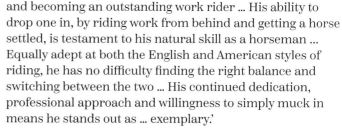

and becoming an outstanding work rider ... His ability to drop one in, by riding work from behind and getting a horse settled, is testament to his natural skill as a horseman ... Equally adept at both the English and American styles of riding, he has no difficulty finding the right balance and switching between the two ... His continued dedication, professional approach and willingness to simply muck in means he stands out as ... exemplary.'

Kremlin House Stables are one of the most famous stables in Newmarket. O'Gorman describes his job there this way: 'We're basically there as a teacher, a coach, to train the horses. Simon is obviously there as a trainer; he gives the orders, a rough set of orders to go by ... and that's what we're there for, to carry that through to our best ability ... If we've been riding for a while, we get to know the horses, and they're all different ... and we can go back and tell Simon or whoever what we think ... I used to be mainly used as a pace jockey, which meant that I rode the lead horse to get the pace right. So I would ride a reasonably good horse, but it was basically setting it up for the better horses.' Big-name mounts have included Dubai Millennium, Daylami and Swain. The financial value of expensive horses becomes a secondary issue, however, once O'Gorman has saddled up.

'There are lots of different work riders. There are lots of different Seamuses,' O'Gorman points out as a way of emphasising the paramount importance of teamwork. A work rider's 'primary job is to educate and school the horse up so that he's fit and ready to go to the races with enough education under his belt to be able to perform on the racetrack ... There's a lot of camaraderie about our job, cos you have to; you're out in all sorts of weathers and you're working unsociable hours ... There's a good bunch of guys involved, and girls, obviously ... Once you've done it for so long and you commit to it, then I think it is a dedication. The money's okay ... When you're race riding, yes, the money's good; when you're work riding, the money is okay, it's liveable, but there's nothing spectacular about it. So it is basically a dedication, a way of life, I like to say'.

The work-horse of the riding stable is the work rider, who is responsible for bringing new horses to their peak while teasing and testing the stable's equine charges to their limits

(opposite) Seamus O'Gorman preparing for the day's first ride for Simon Crisford Racing at Kremlin House Stables, and (above) at the gallops on Warren Hill

Sir Mark Prescott

Trainer & owner, Heath House Stables, Newmarket, Suffolk

Sir Mark Prescott is a legend in his own time. A devotee of blood sports including boxing, hare coursing, cock-fighting, bullfighting and hunting, Prescott obtained his first trainer's licence in 1970 and boasts over two thousand winners to his name. Having worked as assistant to the fearsome Jack Waugh, he took over Heath House Stables from Waugh in 1970 (the heath had first been cleared in the 1600s), having spent what he describes as 'the best time of my life' under Waugh's tutelage. When Prescott himself retires, William Butler, who has worked for him for nearly twenty years, is set to take over. Butler, who completed a diploma in Management and Training of Thoroughbred Racehorses, lives near the stables, and an office has been built for him on the premises. The jewel in the stables' crown is 50 miles of grass gallops, with no area of turf used more than once in any year.

Prescott's younger years were somewhat dramatic, to say the least. Having been kicked out of Harrow for putting a whoopee cushion on the preacher's seat on Founder's Day, he broke his back two years later. 'That changed everything,' he muses. In hospital for eighteen months, unable to speak, swallow or blink, he felt like a prisoner in his own body with his mind racing nonstop. It soon became apparent that he would need to live life to the fullest following his recovery.

(opposite) There are famous trainers, and then there is Sir Mark Prescott of Heath House Stables, whose lively reputation matches his legendary achievements in British flat racing over the last fifty years. Prescott has toyed with retirement for a while, 'but not just yet' as he likes to tell his protégé and chosen successor William Butler (left). 'If you don't see me in the arena at 6.15 any morning, you will know I'm officially retired by God!' says Sir Mark

Prescott's approach to training is meticulous; he plans his days down to the last detail. He likens the job of a racehorse trainer to that of a schoolteacher: both are responsible for knowing exactly what their pupils are capable of. His talent and acumen are obvious from the phenomenal successes of such winners as the two-year-old Spindrifter, who won an astonishing thirteen races in one season, and Misty Halo, who won twenty-one of her forty-two races – still a post-war record for a mare.

'I'm not bad now, but I used to be very fiery,' jokes Prescott of his famous temper. 'William's been with me about eighteen years and he's probably only seen me go pop about three or four times.' (Butler counters that he just happened to 'come along at the right time'.) After being thrown out of Harrow, Prescott immediately started a job courtesy of his 'marvellous' stepfather, who found him work with a local trainer, Sid Kernick, who broke in horses that other people could not break. 'The profit from that enabled him to train some racehorses,' Prescott notes, 'but the bread and butter was breaking very difficult horses. So you saw every sort of horse from every sort of background ... With [Kernick] I learned all about horsemanship.' At any one time, Heath House Stables houses no more than fifty horses, thus guaranteeing that each and every one receives individualised attention.

Prescott believes that working with horses requires both experience and intuition. In selecting a racehorse, his reaction is simple: either 'I like him' or 'I don't like him'. 'It's a very personal thing,' he explains. 'It's interesting that for the sort of people who have a higher success rate in buying racehorses, I would think it's a combination of being intuitive and maybe a slice of luck as well ... The difference between the really successful buyer and the fellow who just does all right is probably 5 per cent ... But somebody with that flair can do it. I can think in my lifetime of two or three people who bought horses. They bought a horse I didn't really like, and I would follow it with interest, and very often they were right. I think they just have a feel ... We are never going to get it quite down to simple mathematics.'

Having just finished writing a book about hare coursing, Prescott has 'got things stacked up I'd like to get done [following retirement]. Being a racehorse trainer, you never can.' A black-and-white film buff, he says he sympathises with the eponymous hero of *Citizen Kane*. A man with wide-ranging enthusiasms, he credits his mother, who was a theatre and art critic for *Punch* for thirty-one years (under two pseudonyms), with inspiring an interest in both. But what about relaxing, going on holiday? 'I don't fancy that,' he laughs. 'I don't fancy not getting up.'

(left) Codicil, a three-year-old filly who has won every race she's run, is one of Heath House Stable's special beauties. (above) Some of the stable's fifty horses on parade around the eighteenth-century courtyard, returning from the morning gallops

(right) Sir Mark Prescott reviewing the performance of his horses on Warren Hill in early-morning spring mist. 'It's all about looking for the hidden signs when assessing a horse,' he observes. With over two thousand winners since taking over Heath House Stables in 1970, Prescott's eye is a much-valued commodity in the British horse world

The National Stud

Newmarket, Suffolk

The National Stud was founded by William Hall Walker, son of a wealthy brewer. A soldier, politician (after a lengthy political career, in 1919 he became Lord Wavertree), amateur jockey and polo player, Walker enjoyed considerable success as a breeder prior to gifting his bloodstock to the British government in 1915. His aim was to remedy the country's shortage of thoroughbred stallions in order to breed cavalry remounts and future champions of the turf. Although initially this idea met with a lukewarm response, influential figures with ties to both racing and politics rallied to persuade the government to accept it.

The National Stud's first manager was Captain Henry Greer, who produced high-class staying stock with great success. Peter Burrell, the Stud's longest-standing Director to date, was responsible for the layout of the farm and yards. In 1942, under Burrell, the Stud bred the winners of four of the year's Classics.

In 1963, the decision was made to sell the Stud's mares and act as a stallion station with operations consolidated into a single new facility on 500 acres at Newmarket. The newly established Levy Board was tasked with running the Stud, and the 500 acres were leased from The Jockey Club. Four years later, HM The Queen officially opened the current site. It was not until the 1980s that the Stud's first full-time training programmes started. After the Stud was acquired by The Jockey Club in 2008, thus coming under the governance of a Royal Charter, its commercial operations began acting solely for the good of British horseracing. Having been founded in 1750 by a group of gentlemen brought together by a shared passion for horseracing, The Jockey Club initially met in London at the Star and Garter in Pall Mall and also in James's Street and Hyde Park, soon relocating to Newmarket. Today it is the largest commercial group in British horseracing. Indeed every penny it makes is invested back into racing.

Tim Lane has been stud manager of Newmarket Nursery since 2017. 'We are run by a board and a chairman, the Duke of Roxburghe, and we have eight other board members,' he explains. 'I run it day to day, but they run it with strategies and what have you.' Having grown up with horses, Lane 'rode very badly as an amateur' and worked his way up from the bottom. His busiest time of year runs from January until mid-May. In addition to its permanent residents, the farm boards around 120 horses for a range of clients. 'We have a lot of boarding mares for clients that use stallions [here],' Lane notes, 'so they bring them up when they are in foal. We'll foal them down and get them covered and then head home. We do have permanent boarding mares … We charge a flat rate for mares and foals; it would be about £32 a day for a mare, and without a foal it's £30 a day … We are very well known for boarding mares and doing a good job. There aren't many farms nowadays where they will take boarding mares … Also we use two very, very good vets – world-class vets – so if you have a mare with a bit of a problem, she'll come here and they'll do the work.'

Although Lane puts in long hours, and at busy times of the year is at it seven days a week, he says, 'I work on the theory that if you can get up in the morning and put on a pair of jeans and wellies and earn a good living, it's good. I'm very lucky that I get to work with very good people … When everything is going right, it's great. When everything is going wrong, that's when you see how good people are.'

(left) Tim Lane on inspection rounds in the magnificent grounds of the National Stud. (opposite) A recently born foal, perfect in all its proportions and not yet twelve hours old. Foals are not named until they're bought by new owners, but the sire's (Nayef) and mare's (Gratification) lineage ensure a winning combination

(left) Untappable, the richest filly in the National Stud, out on a walkabout, spring's first buds finally showing at the end of a long winter

(above) Mares and their
foals range freely in the
Stud's lush grass paddocks,
while (left) five champions
including Mill Reef (his
statue just visible in the
background) are buried on
hallowed ground there

The Suffolk Punch

The Suffolk Punch Trust, Hollesley, Suffolk

Known as one of Britain's oldest breeds, the Suffolk horse's history is better documented than that of any of the others. Said to have existed in East Anglia in 1300, the breed was described two hundred years later exactly as we would recognise it today. Almost certainly from Belgium, the pedigrees go back to 1768. By that time, all male lines but one had died out, creating a genetic 'bottleneck'; a second such bottleneck occurred for the Suffolk Punch in the late eighteenth century. About a century later, the Suffolk Horse Society was formed in Britain to promote the breed. When the first Suffolk Horse Stud Book was published in 1880, there were more than fourteen hundred stallions and about eleven hundred mares registered in the UK. By 1908, the Suffolk had been exported to Spain, France, Germany, Austria, Russia, Sweden, various parts of Africa, New Zealand, Australia, Argentina and elsewhere.

Of solid stature and always chestnut in colour, with minimal white markings generally found on the head and legs, these horses are intended for strenuous tasks such as cart-pulling. Known to be energetic and nimble for a horse of its physique, the Suffolk Punch's population was badly dented during World War I, when thousands died attempting to haul heavy artillery towards the trenches. While their numbers steadily recovered during the 1920s, the introduction of tractors saw another steep decline from the 1960s onwards, with the breed now considered to be the rarest horse in Britain.

In commercial terms, one of the most important uses of the Suffolk horse today is crossing it with thoroughbreds to produce hunters. On the brink of extinction, there are just three to four hundred animals left in the UK, and only seventy-three breeding mares. Genetic samples are being collected from stallions across the globe to ensure enough variance survives to kickstart the breed if traditional methods fail. Although breed technologies are advanced, it is expensive to get a mare to pregnancy, costing around £10,000 to collect semen. Another issue is that the breed's popularity has dropped. To save the horse, its versatility in sports such as hunting and on smaller farms where industrialisation may be too expensive or cumbersome are being publicised. There has also been a rise in the use of Suffolk Punch ladies' carts – two wheeled carts from America.

The Suffolk Punch is a type of draught horse with a storied background. Engineered through cross-breeding in the sixteenth century, these horses (which can weigh up to a ton) are reputed to pull heavy wagons until they drop. The species, in danger of extinction, is being kept alive by the efforts of a few dedicated groups, including the Suffolk Punch Trust. The trust's senior stallion, Besthorpe Achilles (opposite), stands 17 hands high with a massive neck and shoulders, yet has the gentlest disposition. (left) Colt Colony Astall has a long way to grow to match the stud's granddaddy

The Grand National

Aintree Racecourse, Aintree, Liverpool

The history of the Grand National can be traced back to the early 1800s, when the first official races were organised at Aintree. It was Edward William Topham, a respected handicapper, who was responsible for turning the Grand National into a handicap in 1843 after it had been a weight-for-age race for the first four years. The Topham family owned substantial tracts of land around Aintree, and in 1949 they bought the course from Lord Sefton, from whom the land had previously been leased.

The current course, which stages races over conventional fences and hurdles, opened in 1839. A difficult period for Aintree in the post-war years led to it being sold to a property developer. Bookmaker Ladbrokes then stepped in to manage the Grand National until 1984, when Seagram Distillers became sponsors. Famous fences include Becher's Brook, named after Captain Martin Becher, who sheltered in the brook after being unseated. The Chair is the tallest fence, at over 5 feet. A massive nine million people watch the event on television in the UK and another six hundred million around the globe.

The Grand National is Europe's most valuable jump race; by 2014, the prize fund had reached £1 million. The race is popular with viewers who do not normally follow racing or bet on races. The steeplechase has made headlines year after year. Known as the 'ultimate test of horse and rider', the Grand National course differs from that of other National Hunts in that it is run over a longer distance and features much larger fences. The cores of the fences, rebuilt in 2012, are now made from flexible plastic, which is more forgiving than the original wooden-core fences. They are topped with Lake District spruce. All sixteen fences are jumped on the first circuit, but on the second and final circuit, horses bear right onto a run-in for the winning post.

(below left) Pomp and ceremony, and blood and guts, at the 2018 Grand National's Aintree Racecourse, one of the world's most famous and challenging hurdle races. (below right) Tiger Roll jumping the Chair as the other runners thrill the capacity crowds (opposite), racing to an epic photo-finish with Tiger Roll beating second-placed Pleasant Company by a virtual whisker. Europe's most valuable jump race, the Grand National attracts punters from across Britain and the world to watch riders and their mounts risk death for glory (and valuable prize money)

Serena Cookson

Connemara pony breeder, Upper Slaughter, Gloucestershire

Until her grandmother Lady Hemphill's death in 2015, Serena Cookson co-owned studs with her in both the UK and Ireland, focusing on the breeding of Connemara ponies. Having been born in India, where her father served until the 1930s, Lady Hemphill had been breeding and exporting ponies since the early 1960s. The 'Tulira' prefix identified an enterprise that began over dinner with film director John Huston, who mentioned he was selling off his ponies. A deal was done on the spot.

The Connemara pony is known for its stamina and versatility. Connemaras are capable of carrying an adult in the hunt field yet gentle enough for a young child, fearless as a show jumper yet steady as a driving pony. Today there are approximately two thousand foals born in Ireland each year. The consensus is that the history of the breed begins with the arrival of the Celts. Battle was a fundamental component of Celtic life, and pairs of hardy ponies drawing chariots were key to success. The Celts' ponies crossed with the native breed, and their development remained uninterrupted for sixteen centuries. Harsh conditions created an active, sure-footed, clever breed. It is believed that Spanish Barb and Andalusian horses were also imported and that several of these found their way to Connemara, where they were crossed with the native pony breed. More recently, Connemara ponies increasingly began to resemble Arabs.

'When I came to take this stud on, I had so much behind me to go forward with,' muses Serena Cookson. 'That was one of the main reasons why I wanted to keep it going ... I spent a lot of time with my grandmother in Ireland before she died, when she was very well, and my passion grew as my relationship with her grew. I'd always been very close to her, but ... I [also] realised that I had an eye for a horse. I had a lot of my grandmother's instincts and I definitely have her demeanour as well when it comes to people. So it just felt very right.' As far as Ireland's particular importance in the horse world, Cookson points to the fact that some of the best horses come from there, especially in the racing world. 'Huge amounts of horses are imported from Ireland, especially down south,' she notes, 'because they have the lines there and they have the fertility, the ground, and the environment for breeding horses and breeding them well.' She has kept her own breeding in Ireland, noting, 'Why would you take a good French wine out of France where its home is, where it's bred and cultivated? I use this as my selling point.' She emphasises that 'the reason the Connemara is such a substantial pony and so able to cope with the elements is because Ireland's weather is terrible. But then also it's got very good breeding grounds because it's rich in limestone, which is what horses need.' She cites temperament as the breed's outstanding quality: 'Most of them will do any kind of job [and] they have this ability to just be calm.'

'There's a famous saying, and my grandmother always said to me, "Fools breed for wise men to buy,"' Cookson notes. 'It's one of the biggest truths as a breeder that I've experienced. At the end of the day, it's an eleven-month gestation period: you cover a mare with a stallion, God knows what you're going to get at the other end, so really as a breeder – of ponies, not horses – I'm not selling these things for millions like in the racing world. It's more just keeping yourself going rather than making more in a casino. So actually, [even though] I've always had that saying with me, I sort of go against it because it's my passion. The thing is, we've got sixty years of our bloodlines, so that's why my dream is, now they're in my hands, to be able to continue what's been successful for so long. Can I give it another sixty years of success? That's my wish. Because it really is hard.'

(below) Tulira Robuck, a four-year-old Connemara gelding, and (opposite) Serena Cookson with Tulira Darog, a beautiful Connemara stallion which she bred herself, pictured in the gardens of her parents' home

Tulira Darog (left), a prize
Connemara stallion, being
prepared (teased by a mare
on heat) for mating (above).
Always a high-stakes process
fraught with the risk of
failure or injury, modern-day
breeding is huge business
during the season (May
through August). (opposite)
The stallion is successfully
shepherded to its mount in
the presence of a vet, two
assistants, a stable hand
and breeder Serena Cookson
(outside the frame)

Charlie Mann

Racehorse trainer, Neardown, Upper Lambourn, Berkshire

'I came to Lambourn in 1979 to work for Nicky Henderson as a conditional jockey,' explains flamboyant horseman Charlie Mann. 'I rode for seventeen years, and I broke my neck in 1989, in a race at Warwick. That finished my career as a jockey. I [then] spent three years outside of racing. I started a dealing company that didn't really get off the ground, decided I wasn't qualified to do it, and so I became a racehorse trainer ... in 1993. I actually rode in a race in 1994, a race called the Pardubice, which I couldn't get a licence for because ... I had broken my neck. So I printed my own licence!' Mann adds, by way of understatement, 'I've had a fairly colourful life ... I got locked up in a Czech jail for standing on the back of a car going up a motorway ... I was trying to impress a girl, actually. I rode in the Pardubice to impress another girl ... I had seven houses in Lambourn

at one stage. Then the tax man got hold of me and I had to sell all of them to pay a tax bill. I've dealt in cars, in caviar, in watches.' What Mann does not say is that the Great Pardubice Steeplechase is the most difficult and oldest cross-country race in Europe, held annually in the Czech Republic since 1874. The track is more than 4 miles in length and includes thirty-one obstacles. The most fearsome of these, the Taxis Ditch, may be jumped only once a year, in October during the race. Horsemen and -women like Mann gravitate towards challenging courses like the Pardubice in pursuit of the most dangerous adventures the world of horses can offer up.

Of his current, more sedate establishment (Charlie Mann Racing), the adventurer says, 'This yard has worked very well. We really are trying to get back to where we were, although we had a good season this year and a good season last year. It's difficult because you're either in fashion or you're out. It's a very competitive business right now.' Having been voted the year's most eligible bachelor in 1995, Mann works with his fiancée Kate Tierney, and has trained more than eight hundred winners at every level over jumps. Stressing the importance of maintaining personal relationships with owners, he is constantly on the phone letting them know how their horses are doing.

Mann describes his purpose-built yard as a five-star horse hotel emphasising every aspect of 'care and attention'. Situated near the foot of the gallops in Upper Lambourn, the facilities include turnout paddocks and pens, a covered horse walker, weighing scales, a solarium, stabling for forty-four horses, a range of schooling fences, and access to a 5-furlong track (cushion track) and all-weather gallop.

(left) Charlie Mann keeping a close eye on the stable's morning activities, and on his fiancée Kate. (opposite) Mann with The Lion Dancer, one of his favourite charges

The Stable Lass

Roisin Kinney, Charlie Mann Racing, Neardown, Upper Lambourn, Berkshire

Stable lasses/lads work in horseracing yards, where they normally live (or nearby) and sometimes are offered free stabling for their own horses. There are no entry requirements for the job, but positions are often given to teenagers fresh out of racing college, assistant grooms or apprentices. Duties can include (among other things) responsibility for stable staff and horses in the yard, replacing horses' bedding, cleaning equipment, mucking out stables and treating minor wounds. In studs and breeding yards, stable lasses work with stallions, mares and foals, at times assisting vets.

In her twenties, Irish stable lass Roisin Kinney describes her job this way: 'It involves starting work at 6.00 in the morning, mucking out your horses; it involves grooming them, so giving them a brush, riding them out, doing bits of work, coming back, feeding them and making sure they're all right, rugging them up; it also involves going racing with them.' Her father, who loves horses, used to take her to race meetings, which is where Kinney realised she wanted to be a jockey. Before taking up riding, she qualified as an Outdoor Pursuits Instructor, doing mountaineering, kayaking and other rugged sports.

'Every horse is different,' Kinney observes. 'You can tell by the way it stands, if it looks at anything, you can feel it underneath you ... If you show any sort of fear, the horse will know.' At which point, absolutely anything can happen. Her worst experience involved a horse breaking its leg while she was riding it. 'We were just cruising on up one of the gallops – I had two furlongs left to go – and its front fetlock snapped. Just as soon as I heard it, I went to jump [off], but obviously it was a quick thing that happened ... You can't really pull it up if you're going that fast ... It came down and took me with it, so I was sort of underneath it ... I was very badly concussed cos I cracked my helmet and I tore ligaments in one of my ankles ... It was just a freak accident – there was a shoe in the gallop and I didn't see it and it went through his foot.' The horse had to be shot. Kinney was meant to take three weeks off, 'but because it's racing, I don't really like taking days off. You want to show that you're keen if you want to get anywhere ... So I went back into work the next day.'

'Not everyone is a good rider, as much as you can try telling someone what to do,' the stable lass explains. 'It's how someone finds out how to do it themselves. It's having good horsemanship skills ... A lot of people just put their stirrups up as high as they can, trying to get a nice position, looking good, and just cantering round, galloping, going flat out. Other people like myself ride as long as I can, trying to get to know the horse and trying to work it to the best of its ability. If I was on a horse that just wanted to go flat out all the time and it just kept on trying to run away with me, instead of cantering straight, I'd put my stirrups down long and canter it in circles, and every time it tried to do something I didn't ask it to, I would pull it back into a walk and stop it ... If they're trying to do what they want to do ... it's best if you try and pull it back, stop it or take it back into a walk, and then, whenever you're ready, give it a nudge when to go again but at the pace you want it to go at.'

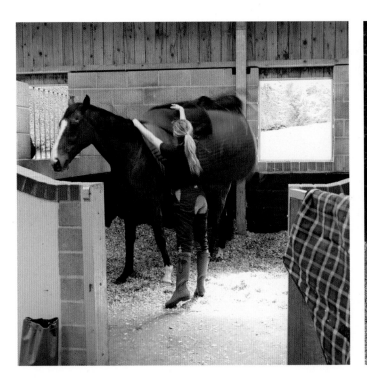

(opposite) Roisin Kinney and Morney Wing. (far left) Kinney cleaning out the stables, and (left) with Pickamix on a walk around the grounds

(following spread) The English spring's second calling as bluebells appear out of nowhere to carpet select woodland in late April and early May. They are mostly hidden from view, but once found, the sight is a balm for the weary traveller, making any journey worth the effort

Anthony Ernest Oppenheimer
Breeder & racehorse owner, Hascombe Stud, Newmarket, Suffolk

Anthony Ernest Oppenheimer was born in 1937 into the diamond-company empire De Beers. His father, Sir Philip Oppenheimer, an avid racehorse enthusiast, had famously overseen the strict control of global diamond supplies intended to end the wild price swings that had led to the failure of many diamond mines in the early 1900s. Internationally known for his involvement in horseracing in Britain, Sir Philip owned a stable and was one of the country's most successful home-based owner-breeders. Elected to The Jockey Club in 1971, he arranged for De Beers to sponsor the King George VI and Queen Elizabeth Diamond Stakes at Ascot. Then, having purchased Hascombe Stud in 1965, he merged it with his own Valiant Stud. Anthony himself has served the De Beers Group in several capacities, as well as being Director of Hascombe & Valiant Stud Ltd since 2015. Stellar horses he has owned (whether outright or as part of a syndicate) have included Golden Horn (in a one-year racing career in 2015, he won seven of his nine races, including the Prix de l'Arc de Triomphe and the Derby); Cracksman (the highest-rated horse in Europe in 2017, who, the following year, enjoyed a stunning win in the Prix Ganay at Longchamp); and Shergar (the world's most famous, most valuable racehorse at the time, who won the 1981 Epsom Derby by ten lengths, the longest winning margin in the race's 202-year history). Kidnapped by the IRA in 1983 and presumed killed the same year, Shergar became the stuff of legend in the racing world.

Anthony Ernest Oppenheimer (left) at Hascombe Stud's stable entrance; the compound was originally built in 1937. (opposite) Golden Horn, Oppenheimer's prized stallion, who won both the Derby and the Arc de Triomphe in 2015. The horse, now at stud, commands a high price for his services, with up to five mountings a day during the breeding season (May to August)

'My introduction to the horse was basically when I was about fifteen,' recalls Oppenheimer. 'I was taken by my parents ... to my grandmother to learn to ride, with a certain Captain Justin of the 11th Hussars in an indoor riding school ... I absolutely hated it ... Captain Justin was a brilliant horseman, but for a fifteen-year-old boy, all I wanted to do was gallop ... I had to do dressage all the time, keep my feet in and everything ... and a couple of jumps, and back I went into the car. I did this a few times, and everyone realised it just wasn't working.' When Oppenheimer joined the 11th Hussars himself, everything changed. 'They were very much a cavalry regiment,' he explains. 'Virtually all my friends ... spent a huge amount of time riding, in National Hunt chases and cross-country. So I often went with them. Gradually I enjoyed it more and more ... I used to go racing with them, on all the northern racecourses ... And then suddenly, my father – out of the blue after the war – came down to Newmarket and bought four horses ... with a couple of Irish friends of his ... and these four horses were put into training with Charlie Elliot ... [My father] had been at Cambridge, and one of his best friends there, Nicky Morriss at Banstead Manor Stud ... said to my father, "Why don't we join up a little bit?" ... We had one or two mares there ... and shared a couple of horses in training, and so my father began to learn a lot more about horseracing.' When Morriss died tragically and his son took over the stud, Sir Philip decided to purchase a stud of his own, 'lock, stock and barrel ... So it was a big learning lesson'. A decade later, Oppenheimer became his father's business partner.

As a breeder, Oppenheimer has always enjoyed the excitement of choosing the right horse for the right mare. He credits his former mother-in-law with having 'a fantastic eye for a horse, a really good eye. We used to go around all the studs in England but mainly Ireland, France and America'. All the while he was still working for De Beers, so his holidays were spent looking at horses and gradually building up the stud. When speaking about Golden Horn, however, he claims all the credit for the horse's success: 'I did the mating, I earned the mare ... [Golden Horn] is earning at the moment £60,000 a go. Say he covers a hundred mares, so I would guess a hundred mares in foal, so each one costs £60,000. I split that with the Sheik [Mohammed bin Rashid Al-Maktoum, owner of the Darley thoroughbred stallion operation] so he gets half of the income and I get half. It comes to about a couple of million into the stud. Which turns the stud around, to make it profitable.' More business-minded than his father where horses are concerned, Oppenheimer's commercial instinct has made it possible to keep the stud in the black. 'Well,' he adds, 'now it's got Golden Horn's income and obviously he's insured too. If Cracksman goes into stud and everything goes right, we'll probably have Cracksman's income too.' What advice would he give his children? 'Cut down a little bit and keep using top-quality stallions, so have fewer horses but more quality.'

(opposite left) Token of Love and Palitana, month-old foals, enjoying each other's company in the warm spring sunshine, while (opposite right) a filly stays close to her mother in their paddock. (right) Steven Golding, assistant stud manager, leads a foal and mare from stable to paddocks. Golding has been working at Hascombe for more than thirty years

Richard Brown

Bloodstock agent, Newmarket, Suffolk

Bloodstock agent Richard Brown purchases and often manages bloodstock (thoroughbred horses). 'I buy mares in foal, I buy foals, I buy yearlings – horses that are one year old – two-year-olds, horses in training – anything that is a thoroughbred, i.e. a racehorse, I buy and then subsequently manage,' he explains. 'It means that from the moment the hammer comes down and I sign the ticket, I make sure that the horse goes to the right trainer, goes to the right place ... You've got pedigree and you've got bloodlines that are obviously more desirable than others, but a good horse can come from anywhere. What we do, it's not a science, it is an art ... It's about the horse's movement, it's about the way that the horse is put together. For me it's like a jigsaw puzzle. How does the shoulder fit into the neck? How does the hind end fit into the middle? How much heart room has the horse got? What's its eye like? How does it behave? A big thing for me is temperament. These horses are going to have to go through the pain barrier for you. If they're not very happy at the sales, they're swishing their tail, they're very unlikely, when the sticks are up in a year's time and they've got to go through the pain barrier to get to the winning post first, they're unlikely to do it. So you're piecing this all together. You're then including pedigree – where the horse has come from – and that then forms a shortlist of what you're going to try. Then it obviously becomes price dependent. Certain clients have different budgets, and we always set a limit on how far we're going to go on every horse, like you would at every auction.'

As with human beings, so with horses, says Brown. 'If you look through history, a lot of the real geniuses have had major quirks. And a lot of the very brightest people in history have the most talent.' The most significant difference, he feels, is that 'if you're a human athlete, you are trained; you content yourself to go through the pain barrier cos you know what the reward is. If you're a horse, you have to coerce them through the pain barrier, cos they don't know; you can't explain that if you go fast here for another hundred yards, you're going to win the guineas and you'll get to shag two hundred mares a year for the rest of your life!' Being leader of the pack is critical to equine success. 'If you go to a field of any horses, not just thoroughbreds, you will see ... more of sort of an aggressor, a boss,' Brown notes. 'All the mares are turned out together; all the stallions are obviously kept on their own cos if you put them together, they fight like hell and they're too valuable. Whenever you put a very good race mare in a paddock of mares, she's almost always the boss. She's almost always the dominant female ... So yeah, they have to have personality, character and mental toughness. But it has to be within control.' Most good horses, Brown believes, 'are quite quirky and they're quite highly strung, so it's not like when you're at the sales you're looking for a steady plodder. You are looking for something with a bit of spark, but it's got to be that spark that can be contained, cos if they're too mad, you won't be able to train it'.

Brown's advice to a potential purchaser is honest and clear: 'Look, you've bought your yacht, and that's probably not going to lose a huge amount of money and you're going to be able to enjoy it every day. You've bought your art, and if you've bought it right, it's going to go up in value. You're now going to buy your horse, and it's almost certainly going to lose you money. They are very expensive. A yacht can sit in a dry dock and get looked at once a year. A horse needs to be fed three times a day, it needs to be mucked out twice a day, it needs to be ridden out. They cost an enormous amount of money in the first place and then they cost a lot of money to maintain. So I'd be saying to you, "You'll get a far bigger high having a winner than you would going on your yacht or looking at your art ... but if you've come to me at this point ... do not think that you will get a return from this; this will cost you money." There is a chance, but I would never sell racing horses as an investment.'

Racing, of course, has always been the sport of the wealthy. 'Charles II was racing horses here [in Newmarket] in the 1600s,' Brown notes, 'and was racing them against estate owners. In The Jockey Club, they used to race each other for estates. So I would meet you and I'd say, "I've got this horse, he's better than yours," and you'd just have match races. I'd say, "Right, what have you got?" You've got your ten-bedroom house in Kensington. I'd say, "Okay, well, I've got a thousand acres in Scotland. Let's go!"'

It was King James I who introduced the sport to the sleepy village of Newmarket in the early 1600s, and it was during the reign of Charles II that racing flourished and developed. The Jockey Club, founded in 1750 by a group of gentlemen, became Jockey Club Racecourses and then Racecourse Holdings Trust with the purchase of Cheltenham Racecourse to secure the track's future. Soon after, other courses joined the Group, and in 2006, the Horserace Regulatory Authority was formed to take on The Jockey Club's role of policing the sport. For much of its existence, many of its members divided their time between Parliament and conducting racing's affairs from The Jockey Club Rooms. The Morning Room, considered to be the heart of the club, houses the most important items in its renowned art collection.

Richard Brown (above) in the main dining room of Newmarket's The Jockey Club Rooms. Adorned with silver and gold trophies and memorabilia from three centuries, the Rooms' walls are covered by a unique collection of equine masterpieces by artists from George Stubbs, Alfred Munnings to Sir Edwin Henry Landseer. (left) Brown in one of the booths that served as meeting places for enthusiasts willing to bet their livelihoods on a single race between two horses. (right) Brown gambling at the high-stakes game of buying horseflesh at Tattersalls, the equine auctioneers, dropping £65,000 on an animal that has never run before – a punt based on an expert eye, good horse sense and genealogy

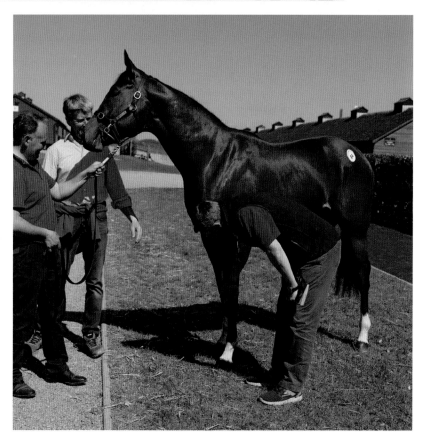

Tattersalls Bloodstock Auctioneers

Newmarket, Suffolk

Tattersalls, the oldest bloodstock auctioneers in the world and the largest in Europe, was founded in 1766 by Richard Tattersall, who left his father's farm in Lancashire to sell horses at Hyde Park Corner in London. The firm moved to Knightsbridge Green in the 1860s and to Newmarket in 1965, having remained a family business until the death of Edmund Somerville Tattersall in 1942. Tattersalls were party to The Jockey Club's production of an industry code of practice.

Over the last thirty years, the quantity and quality of stallions based in Newmarket have increased rapidly, largely due to investment from overseas. The grounds in which the horses are paraded resemble a country-house garden whose focal point is a stone cupola surmounted by the bust of George IV with a fox at its centre – the firm's logo. Maintaining tradition, current Chairman Edmond Mahony runs Tattersalls with the standards and ethos of a family company. Horses can be as valuable as Old Master paintings, but if they fail at auction, their value can plummet to almost nothing. They are assessed by pedigree, physical shape, fluidity and straightness of movement, and are sold in guineas (a guinea is £1.05), with the company keeping 5 per cent on every transaction. Buyers come from more than fifty countries, and every Tattersalls sale in 2017 achieved record figures.

Marketing Director Jimmy George explains that 'the main racing and breeding countries in Europe are Britain, Ireland and France,' with 'the biggest single breeding and racing country in the world [being] America'. In 2017 Tattersalls 'sold approximately £350 million worth of thoroughbreds', he adds. 'The record price ever sold here for an individual horse is 6 million guineas and that was ... last December for a lovely filly called Marsha. She was a race filly ... owned by a big syndicate called Elite Racing and she was top-class ... one of the best sprinters of her generation, well bred, very good looking ... The average price last year ... here at Tatts in Newmarket was around the 65,000-guinea mark.' Asked who the big buyers are, George explains, 'The amazing thing about the thoroughbred business and racehorse ownership is it's not just for the very, very wealthy. I think sometimes it's perceived that way, but you can buy a thoroughbred here for as little as 800 guineas or for as much as 6 million. Everybody comes here with the same intention, and that's to buy themselves a champion in one shape or form ... The only thing that separates people here is how much money they've got, not what they're trying to buy.' Today microchipping is used to check horses' identification, verify parentage and markings. 'So it's rigorous; it has to be,' George notes.

'Public auction is very theatrical, particularly at the top level,' George observes. 'There's not a huge amount of glamour associated with every sale that we stage here, but the top sales, yeah, it's great theatre, it's fairly compulsive viewing. There was a two- to three-hour period at the December sale last year, surrounding that sale of the filly we mentioned earlier called Marsha, where I think the average price in that three-hour period was about 600,000 guineas, and there was an awful lot of money changed hands in that three hours. It's hugely exciting, it's proper theatre, but there's serious stuff going on at the same time. This is a business as well as a sport ... During the sales there are hundreds of people here. Car parks are full, there are people busy working but busy enjoying themselves as well ... Our longest sale would be twelve days, so people could end up finding themselves spending an awful lot of time at Tattersalls during our sale season. You have to have the facilities to go with that.'

Tattersalls is a must-visit for every breeder, bloodstock agent, trainer and racing enthusiast in the country. Founded in 1776, the company's turnover was over £350 million last year. Horses are valuable commodities, yet failure at auction will see their value plummet. But not in the case of this two-year old bay colt (opposite), which fetched the top price of 900,000 guineas. (above) Prime horseflesh on the fly, being put through its paces in the May 2018 sales. This two-year-old bay colt, despite its magnificent bearing, only managed 200,000 guineas at the sale

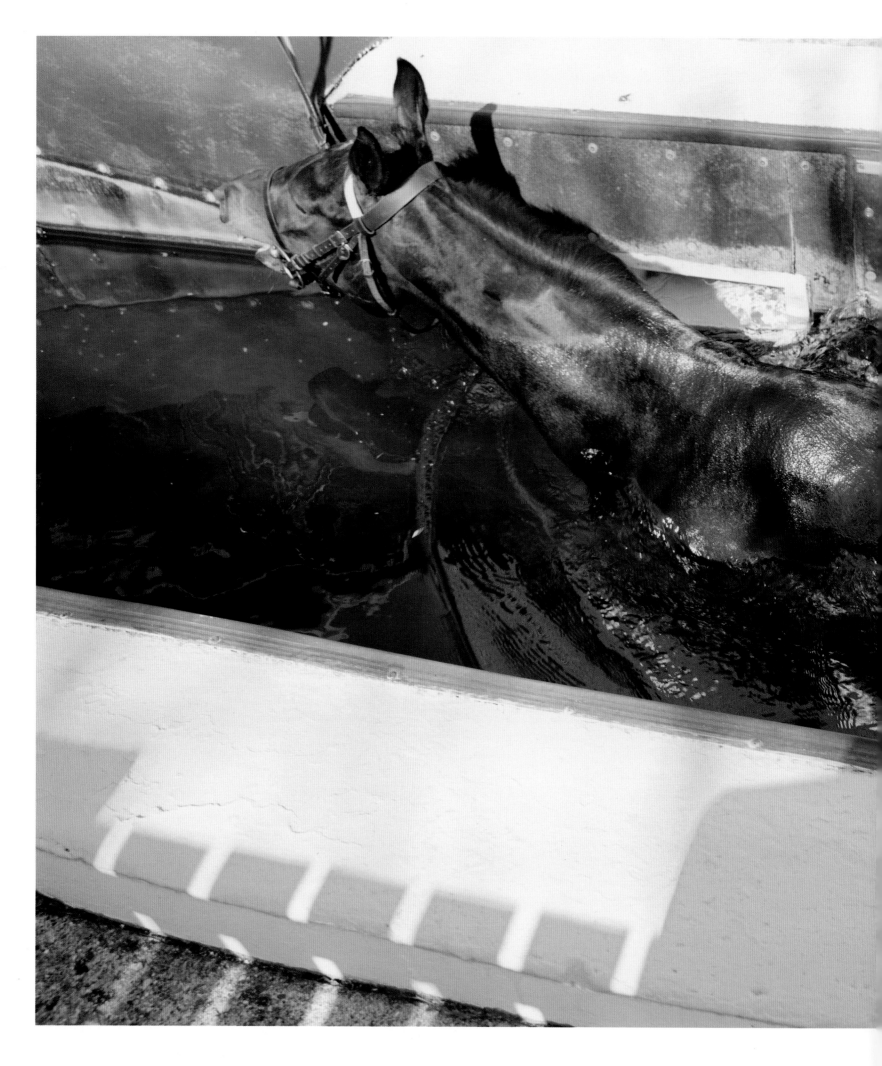

(left) Trouble and Strife enjoying a dip far from the madding crowd in Heath House Stables' equine swimming pool, a luxury on a warm spring day but a necessity for exercising horses most days of the year

The Eriskay Pony

Jemma Lucas, Equine specialist & breeder, Greenlands Stud Farm, Devizes, Wiltshire

Family-run Greenland Stud Farm is a rare-breed stud for Eriskay ponies; owner Jemma Lucas (her husband is former England polo player James Lucas) is an Eagala-qualified equine specialist who works with children and horses. The Eagala method promotes physical, occupational and emotional growth in people suffering from anxiety, autism, cerebral palsy, depression and developmental delay. Equine therapy is highly beneficial to children with autism, helping them develop the core skills they need.

Wild Eriskay ponies, an ancient Hebridean breed, were used by crofters to carry peat and seaweed until the mid-nineteenth century. Usually grey, they are known for their stamina, being able to ride and plough. As with other native pony breeds, the onset of mechanisation, and a decline in population as people migrated, caused numbers to decline. A conservation initiative was launched, and with the help of the last remaining stallion, numbers have gradually risen. There are now 420 known ponies with Eriskay blood across the UK. 'Any ponies that didn't have a good temperament (because they worked with the children and the wives; the husbands were away working) ... were used as a tool for work. They had to be tough, hardy, survive on next to nothing,' notes Lucas. 'They've got waterproof coats and slow-growing hooves so that makes them very practical.' An autism expert, Lucas works alongside a doctor. 'The ponies are free in the arena,' she explains. 'We don't tell people how to sort themselves out or improve their lives; we use the ponies as metaphors, as things that relate to their lives, and the ponies help them find the answers to their questions ... The horses are the mirror, so they will tell me what I need to know about the people without them telling me ... Then I know how to progress the session.'

'I'm a really shy person,' Lucas continues. 'I don't want any sort of limelight on me at all, I want the limelight on the ponies ... We got these boys, they were born here on this farm, I trained them by leading them around the orchard on their own, they went off and they're out there now ... People are talking about them.' Her commitment to equine therapy grew out of the fact that two of her own children were autistic. 'My great-grandfather founded Millfield School in Somerset, and he always said that there's something amazing in everybody, you've just got to find it,' Lucas notes. 'I wanted to find solutions. All my boys have been at mainstream school, mainstream college, and they're flourishing. So they've gone from being really severe to mainstream, to the extent where my seventeen-year-old has had his label taken away now ... Having been in a children's home and a foster home for part of my childhood, I just really wanted to aim for the stars ... Horses were always there for me, whatever I went through in my life. Just a day with a horse, or an hour, you feel so much better. It all incorporated together, with my journey of my childhood, my own children ... That all made this wonderful cake, which is me promoting these ponies which are so incredible for the work that I want to do.'

(left) Jemma Lucas with her prize Eriskay stallions Olympic Gold (white pony) and Twilight, attended by her groom Maddy Collins. (opposite) Lucas, who is married to former England polo-team captain James Lucas, breeds both the endangered Eriskay and polo ponies

(right) Neil Hammond and his nine-year-old daughter Sidney out riding in the bright spring sunshine against a glowing backdrop of rape fields near Wormington, Worcestershire. Sidney, here with Beck, her purebred Dartmoor pony, has been riding since the age of three

Badminton Horse Trials

Badminton, South Gloucestershire

The dukedom of Beaufort was created in 1682, granted to Henry, 3rd Marquess of Worcester in reward for his service to the Stuart monarchy. The Manor of Badminton was purchased by the Worcesters in 1608, and the house as it is today dates from the 1600s and 1700s. Noted architect William Kent completed the north front, giving it its Palladian appearance.

Badminton House is now the family home of the 12th Duke of Beaufort, Harry Somerset, who takes an active role in the trials. His father David, who passed away in 2017, was President of the trials and himself a successful rider. It was the 10th Duke who came up with the idea of hosting an annual equestrian event, believing that Badminton could be used as a training ground for British riders wanting to compete at an international level.

Badminton was first held in 1949, with twenty-two horses entered from Britain and Ireland and some five hundred spectators. For the first ten years, the dressage and show-jumping arenas were sited on the old cricket ground in front of Badminton House. But in 1959, torrential rain turned the park into a sea of mud, so the arenas and tradestands were moved to the present site. The trials were relocated to Windsor in 1955 at the invitation of HM The Queen, and the 2nd European Championships were held there, but the following year they were moved back to Gloucestershire. An outbreak of foot-and-mouth disease forced cancellation in 2001.

The trials are noted for their nail-biting high drama. Total prize money for the three-day event is roughly £360,000. The record for most completions at Badminton (thirty-seven) is held by Andrew Nicholson of New Zealand, who finally won in 2017. Described by *Country Life* as 'one of Britain's greatest sporting traditions' and currently called The Mitsubishi Motors Badminton Horse Trails, the 2018 event hosted over five hundred tradestands, with more than two hundred thousand spectators flocking to watch show jumping, dressage and cross-country. As first-place winner Jonelle Price put it, 'There is nothing quite like winning, and to do it here is very special.' The 2018 cross-country course was designed by Eric Winter, who reversed the direction in which it had been run the previous year. With a combination of a wet spring (causing tiring ground conditions) and warm weather, the expected time proved impossible to make. Despite the difficulties, 74 per cent completed the course and there was only one serious horse injury.

'If you bring a horse to Badminton, it has to be a cross-country horse; it has to want to curl over a fence and jump a little bounce into something, be able to be really neat in front and be brave, get the trip and be able to handle terrain,' notes *Horse & Hound*. Falls are not unusual, with riders having to be airlifted to hospital (in 2017 Emily Gilruth suffered a traumatic brain injury; she has since recovered). Andrew Nicholson, the 2017 defending champion, had suffered a bad fall in 2015 and broken his neck. This did not stop him from winning, on the eighteen-year-old 'campaigner' Nereo.

The Badminton Horse Trials encapsulate British equine tradition in both its quirkiness and the high standards of horsemanship required for anyone to complete the course without breaking their neck or their horse's back. As if to prove the point, James O'Haire of Ireland (right) takes a tumble into the lake at the 2018 trials, his horse inappropriately named China Doll. Ben Hobday (opposite top) braving the Fallen Tree jump. More sedate and less dangerous but equally challenging is the dressage phase of Badminton, in which Nana Dalton (opposite bottom) rode Absolut Opposition against stiff competition

Sabina St John

Horsewoman & fashionista, Chelsea, London

Show jumper Sabina St John is a partner at Tomasz Starzewski Fashion & Interior in London. Her father owned a slaughterhouse in Hamburg. When St John visited and 'heard the animals scream', she 'was quite shaken by it' and became a vegetarian. At the age of nineteen, she arrived in London to work as a model but realised that she did not find the emphasis on outward appearance particularly rewarding, so she enrolled at the European Business School in London. She went on to study and work in several European cities and in Canada as a trader. Having 'always felt a connection with animals', especially horses, she had taken riding lessons in secret (her mother had had a riding accident and would not let St John ride, 'full stop'). Why horses? 'I wanted the soul-connection with the horse, the joy I always felt when I was on horseback ... and yes, I wanted to

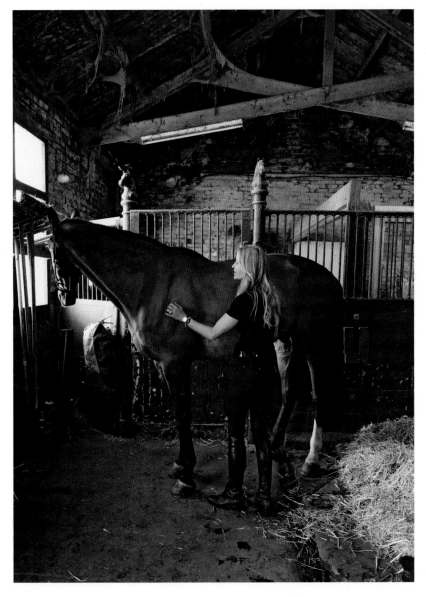

become a good show jumper, I wanted to own horses, I wanted to be in that world, always.'

St John became seriously involved with horses through her ex-husband Donald McTaggart, who owned an equestrian yard. 'After my day in the bank, I would drive out for an hour to ride my horse and then come back to London,' she explains. She and McTaggart 'started expanding what was part of the equestrian school into a competition yard. 'I would say that it was one of the best competition yards in England, because it was so close to London and very professionally run,' says St John. As an amateur rider, she 'did Hickstead and also jumped in Arezzo in Italy ... It was great fun and we had some good success there too'. However, it became difficult to take things to the next level what with 'so many children and a new husband and ... a career in property ... I tend to do more the local shows'.

Extremely close for many years to her business partner Tomasz Starzewski, St John says, 'I don't want to say [I am his] muse ... but it is a little bit like that ... We bounce ideas off of each other and yes, I wear a lot of his clothes.' She still manages to ride four or five times a week, 'religiously'. Of her horses, she adds, 'My gratitude really knows no end ... Not only is it my sport; they ... have saved me many times in my life ... Each time when I was at a low ebb ... I went to my horses and I rode, and they gave me this love and this harmony and a pure, pure energy that each and every time made me feel better ... I had a very severe accident fourteen or fifteen years ago now where I nearly lost my arm ... I had it put back together ... Then for six months I had no nerves, because my nerves had been cut, so I visualised every day that my arm was fully functional, that I could ride my horses ... My horses helped me in this healing process I can't even tell you how much.'

(left) Sabina, Lady St John of Bletso grooming Dani, an English warmblood gelding who is her favoured mount. St John drives over an hour each way from London to Greenacres Equestrian stables in Harpenden, Hertfordshire most days of the week. St John with Dani at work (opposite) and at play in the hay barn (following spread), kitted out in a Tomasz Starzewski ballgown

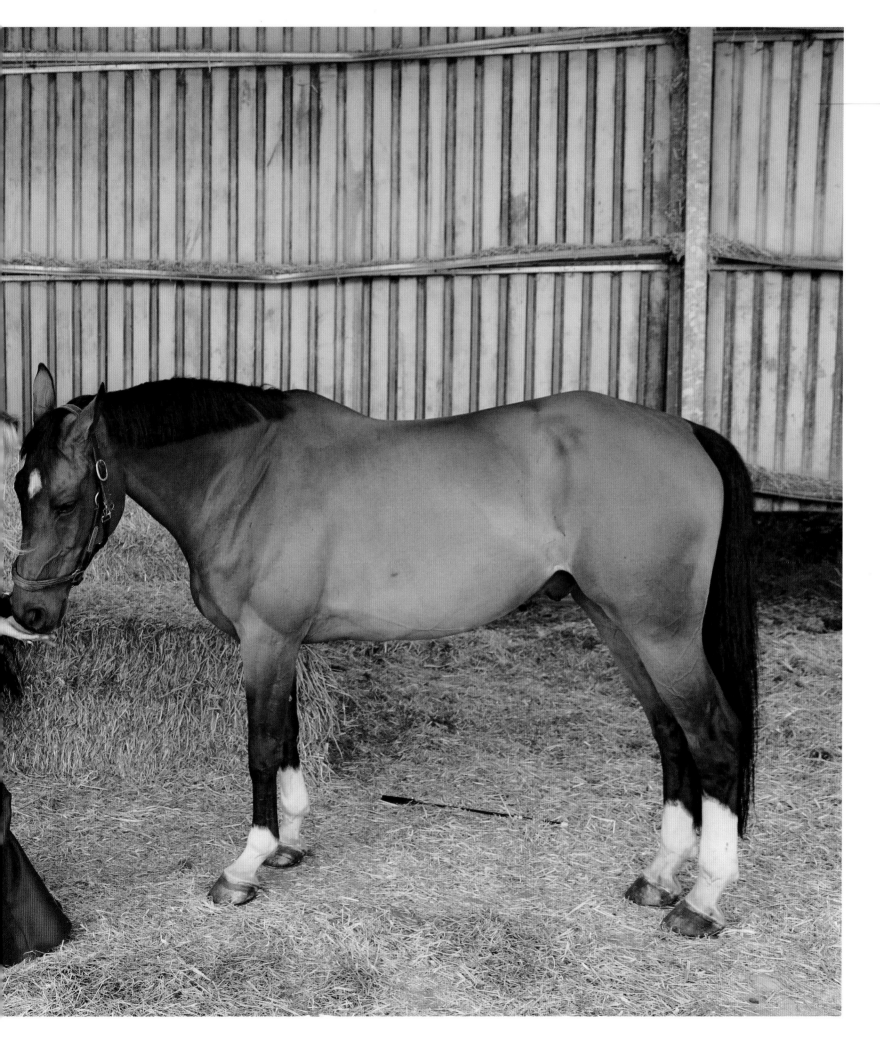

Highclere Stud
John, Carolyn & Jake Warren, Owners, Burghclere, Newbury, Berkshire

Under its original name, Siddown Warren Stud, Highclere Stud was established by the 5th Earl of Carnarvon in 1902. The 6th Earl, a well-known amateur jockey in the 1930s, bought success to Highclere by importing yearlings from the US. However, it was the 7th Earl who truly developed the bloodlines. The Hon Harry Herbert, younger brother of the current Earl, runs the most successful racing syndicate in the world, Highclere Thoroughbred Racing Ltd, of which John Warren is also a Director.

Highclere Stud covers 300 acres of grassland, including both flat and undulating paddocks. John Warren, a greengrocer's son from Essex, is the first man without a title or military rank to become HM The Queen's racing adviser and bloodstock manager. In 1992 he set up Highclere Thoroughbred Racing Ltd, which offers shares in a range of syndicates each summer, with Herbert, who is his brother-in-law. Each shareowner enters into an agreement to share the prize money and proceeds from the sale of the horses once the syndicate is wound up. Syndicates generally last for a minimum of two seasons. Warren is responsible for buying all of the yearlings; to date he has bought group winners for HM The Queen, Sheikh Mohammed bin Maktoum Al-Maktoum, and the dukes of Devonshire and Roxburghe. His wife Lady Carolyn Warren has managed the welfare of the horses at the stud for the last twenty years, and their son Jake is now involved in the business, having spent two years working for sports agency Pitch London.

'It would be a hard business to be involved in if you didn't have the passion to go with it,' says Lady Carolyn of the stud. 'When you explain the business model to some people, it's hard because you're dealing with an animal; there's an element of chance involved ... There's no big sugar daddy sitting here and supporting us, so we have to run this place as a business. Which means all aspects of it, involving everybody ... putting their whole life's work into this place.' Her husband adds, 'Obviously Carolyn and I have been doing it for a very long time. As they say, "When your skin's in it, it counts." Therefore when you have an investment like we do here, you're very focused on the outcome ... Our strategising that we've developed over thirty years of marriage, business and working together is now being passed on to Jake. He's got a natural sense of it. It's one thing being educated and it's another to be natural.'

Highclere was a cattle farm before it was laid down to develop thoroughbreds. 'So we've inherited a lot of history and infrastructure,' John explains. 'We're enhancing it and moving it on to the modern-day bloodlines ... The great thing about horses is that every horse teaches you something new.' John initially came into the equation as a bloodstock agent. 'The previous owners of Highclere Stud were not in that training environment,' he notes. 'I came with that bloodstock point of view, which threw a commercial side into an owner-breeder's environment and is helping us to develop it to go forward.' Meanwhile the syndicate he runs with his brother-in-law 'is known to be probably the most successful syndicate that there is. I do all the selecting for Harry; he does all the management, gets the owners together, creates the syndicates and pulls in the ownership ... Then I go off to the auctions, do the pre-looking; then Harry joins me at the auctions and helps in the selection process ... That has reaped a significant number of top-quality horses'.

Of his own move into the family business, Jake Warren says, 'I was in a position where I could get a job quite readily ... and I started to realise that I knew a lot more than I thought I did ... When it's on your doorstep, sometimes you don't recognise things. You're not entirely sure if there are other things out there that might be for you or that you might prefer.' Being away from his parents in Australia 'kick-started something inside to make me think I was capable of doing it and enjoyed it. So when I came back [to the UK], I got more involved'. While at the University of Edinburgh, he dipped his toe in the water by setting up a small-scale syndicate with some friends. His father says of Jake, 'What will make him into a leader in this industry ... is that he naturally has an opinion. But then it isn't an arrogant opinion; it is rational, sensible and calculated. He never ran away with it thinking he knew things too soon, but he also knew what he liked and what he didn't like. That's when you sense that someone's got a real future.'

(left) The Warrens at Highclere Stud (L–R): John, Lady Carolyn and Jake. Cable Bay (opposite), Highclere's prize stallion, displaying his personality in the grounds. Set among the beautiful rolling Hampshire Downs, Highclere's 300 acres of grassland, paddocks and woodland are located next to Highclere Castle's own thousand acres, the site of the TV series 'Downton Abbey'

(above) The Warren family at work inspecting the 2018 crop of foals and pregnant mares. (opposite) Mare and foal are free to roam in their generous paddock space at Highclere

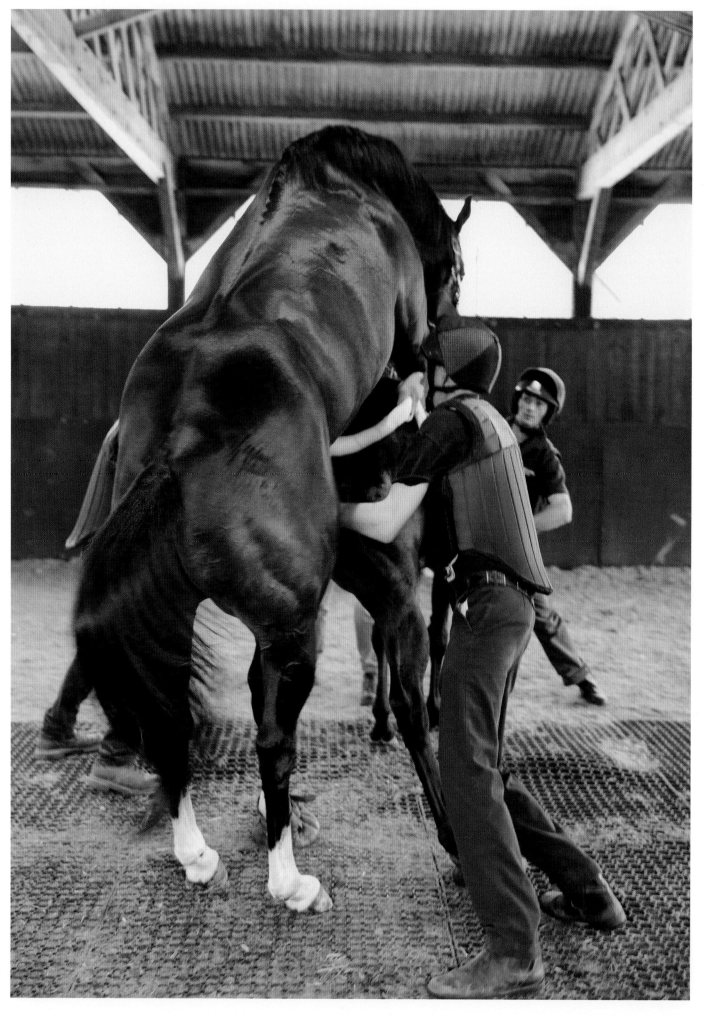

(left) Cable Bay is kept busy during the breeding season, with numerous professionals in attendance to ensure safe passage for both the boisterous stallion and the shy mare brought in from another stud. (opposite) A newly minted colt, evidence of Highclere's successful breeding programme

Major Richard Waygood MBE
Performance manager, Horpit, Wiltshire

A former riding master of the Household Cavalry, Major Richard Waygood MBE has been performance manager for the British dressage squad for a decade. Waygood joined the Army as a private in 1979, was commissioned from the ranks in 2000 and retired from the Household Cavalry in 2008; during this time, he trained and choreographed the Household Cavalry Musical Ride. Waygood became the first serving Army officer in twenty-three years to compete at Badminton, finishing clear and inside the top twenty. He has also won the King's and Queen's Cups on more occasions than any other rider. Not from a horsey family (his father was a gamekeeper), he remembers falling off ponies as a child more often than staying on them.

'I did thirty years altogether and I had the most amazing time,' Waygood says of his time in the Army. 'I joined as a trooper, straight from school at the age of sixteen ... I went to the Guard's Depot in Pirbright ... We did a year's basic training there. I always think of that as a working-class finishing school.' He went on to join the Life Guards: 'We did the first six weeks in riding school, and then on day one of week seven we were told to tack our horses up. We ... rode from London to Windsor [and] did the next ten weeks of riding school in Windsor ... We did a passing-out parade in front of the commanding officer and we rode back into London again.' Quickly realising that he wanted to become a riding instructor, Waygood's other aspiration at the time was to ride around Badminton. Following closely on that was his desire 'to become the Chef d'Equipe/Performance Manager for British Eventing'. Offered the same role for the dressage team instead, he worried because eventing was his forte. 'It was a gamble that fortunately paid off,' he says. 'Having never won any medals at Olympic Games, we won the team gold, individual gold and individual bronze in London, and then we went on to win individual gold and team silver in Rio.'

Waygood attributes his success as a performance manager to 'managing character ... Without character, on the field of play, when you're under pressure, then you fall apart. So you need confidence, you need ambition, you need drive. This is all part of what makes you up ... When you're leading people around who work with horses, often you've got to keep a motivated work force ... If you didn't keep the standards high with the riding staff and the riding instructors, it never kept the standard of equitation high throughout the regiment, and then the horse welfare and management would drop ... So it's discipline, it's motivation, it's giving people a certain amount of ownership.' Of his own career he says, 'Gosh, it's been unique. I've ridden round Badminton, I've ridden across the plains of the Maasai Mara in Kenya, I've galloped with wildebeest, I've ridden across the Thar Desert in India. I've done some amazing things. They are things that you couldn't dream of when I was a fifteen-/sixteen-year-old joining the Army. Never had a clue it would take me on this journey. Imagine doing a job that you're hugely passionate about and you get paid for it at the same time. Amazing!'

(left) Major Richard Waygood, former riding master of the Household Cavalry, attending to stable duties at his horse farm in Wiltshire, and (opposite) showing what Askari, his nine-year-old event horse, is capable of doing on command. As performance manager of the British eventing team, Waygood's command and control are key components of the country's 2020 Olympic hopes

The Devil's Horsemen

Gerard Naprous, Founder, Salden, Buckinghamshire

The Devil's Horsemen, Europe's leading film-industry horse supplier, is owned by French-born Gerard Naprous (considered one of Europe's leading horse masters, stuntmen and stunt coordinators) and his children Daniel and Camilla. Together they provide horses (they stable more than a hundred) of any breed, size or colour; carriages; tack (including dressings from every period and genre); armour; riders and horse wranglers. Their wealth of expertise draws on every equestrian discipline, and their extensive experience allows them to blend disciplines with filming requirements. Live show formats include tailor-made packages for Olympic arenas, county shows, festivals and corporate events.

'As a kid, I became fascinated with all animals and then horses,' says Gerard Naprous. 'I could see a nice way of life in it, although a hard way. My father had a garage but started as a chauffeur ... I rode horses in a riding school ... My first teacher was Polish, from the Polish cavalry of course ... He said, "Gerard, don't stay with me. You have to go from stable to stable to have different teachers and see different ways of riding horses." When I was eighteen, a friend of mine told me he was working on a film. I thought that would be great; dressage is a bit boring ... My first boss was French-Czech ... brought up in Czechoslovakia, where they had a different way of working with horses. He ... was filming a lot in Yugoslavia when [President] Tito left the door open to the American film market. I started with him ... It was a lovely way of life and a nice start.'

Naprous went on to work as a stuntman at the Lido in Paris before arriving in England in 1971 to work with horses onstage. After a short return to Paris, he was back in the UK. 'I came here with £10 that I borrowed from my best friend,' he recalls. 'I opened a café, made some money with that cash loan and bought my first horse.' He then bought horses through some agents, who asked if he would work for them doing jousting and trick riding. He became known in the trade as 'Cavalier du Diable' – The Devil's Horseman. 'In 1986, my son was nine and he used to work with me, already in it; he never really went to school,' Naprous notes. 'We grew and grew ... I bought the first farm with no money, then the next with no money; I was just with the bank. Now, when you say, "Is there money?" I would say, touch wood, "Yes, there is money." Now I have a hundred horses, seven hundred carriages.' In 2016 the company participated in thirty-five productions, among them the hugely popular (and lucrative) *Game of Thrones*.

Naprous' farm covers 150 acres; he employs nearly two hundred people. 'All our big films are American money,' he says. 'We're quite lucky in England because we have the best actors, one of the best crews; we're cheaper for the Americans. We are more efficient. If you do a big movie or a small movie, it's the same. No-one cares who's in it or not in it.' As a Frenchman living in England, he divides his criticism between his birth country and his adopted one. Of the French he says, 'We're very anarchist! ... My dad was self-employed, an artisan. He worked to free France in the war; he got caught by the Gestapo and got away ... Horsemanship in France is still one of the best in Europe [while] English horsemanship is very poor. Right at the top, it's very good. But the English are like that: very good at the top, then very medium. The English always have gold medals and you don't know how. That's the English: they've got this killer instinct at the top.'

(right) Gerard Naprous, master stuntman and founder of the Devil's Horsemen (and an inimitable character straight out of central casting), on a coffee break outside his house set among sprawling grounds, stables, barns, stockrooms and what have you. (opposite) Stuntwoman Emma Thorley sitting pretty on Caravel, a white Lusitano

(right) Naprous showing off his skills on Dante, his favourite horse. (opposite) Naprous, an avid collector of everything to do with horses, inspecting his stock of 850 carriages and carts used in such hit TV series as *Game of Thrones* and *The Crown*

(following spread) Wild horses couldn't keep the author from photographing an action scene by one of the Devil's Horsewomen

Royal Windsor Horse Show
Windsor, Berkshire

The Royal Windsor Horse Show, established in 1943, has run every year since then. Inspired by 'Wings for Victory', Count Robert Orssich and Mr Geoffrey Cross set about organising a horse and dog show to raise money for the war effort. The first one-day event helped the Royal Borough raise £391,197 – enough money to purchase seventy-eight Typhoon fighter aircraft. Competitors had to hack to the showground as there was no petrol to spare. Attended by key members of the royal family including King George VI, Queen Elizabeth The Queen Mother and the two young princesses, Elizabeth and Margaret, it featured the future Queen in the Single Private Driving class, which she won. Since then, she has entered many homebred horses and ponies in various classes. At the first show, a lurcher stole a piece of chicken from the King's plate. The committee was so mortified that they banned dogs from the showground thereafter.

In 1946, the show was extended to two days, with the number of days increasing until 1997 (five days). HRH The Duke of Edinburgh introduced international carriage driving in 1971, going on to win the Horse Teams class in 1982 with HM The Queen's team of bays. Other royal family members who have competed include HRH The Prince of Wales, HRH The Princess Royal and Zara Phillips. Today the show (the largest of its kind in the UK) encompasses a huge variety of equestrian sports, including the Land Rover International Carriage Driving Grand Prix, national and international show-jumping competitions, extensive showing classes and equestrian displays. The Rolex Grand Prix marks the pinnacle of the week's calendar. Money is raised for ABF The Soldiers' Charity and an equestrian charity chosen annually by the committee. The hunter classes are particularly competitive; winning the novice hunter class signals that a young horse has exciting potential. As 2017 winner Kent Farrington put it, 'This is one of my favourite shows … There's a combination of an amazing setting, an unbelievable crowd, top course designing and great footing.'

The Royal Windsor Horse Show (left & opposite) has been a constant in the equine calendar since 1943. Amazing settings (Windsor Castle is next door) and top equestrian course design draw competitors from across the world, and a crowd from both London and the shires

Images of pomp, pageantry and tradition combine to create the most incongruous scenes imaginable. (left) The Household Cavalry's commanding duty officer is attended by his groom in preparation for the arrival of HM The Queen and Prince Philip, while (opposite) numerous coach-and-fours, their occupants dressed to the nines, parade their late nineteenth- and early twentieth-century finery in front of bemused attendees

Tara Wilkinson

Carriage driver, Windsor, Berkshire

(above) Young Tara Wilkinson, champion driver, in her finery by the Thames during practice for the Royal Windsor Horse Show carriage competition

(opposite) Wilkinson accompanied by Floridian carriage-driving enthusiast Misdee Wrigley Miller, a keen horsewoman and one of the heirs to the eponymous chewing-gum empire

Carriage driving is in the Wilkinson family genes, spanning three generations. In fact, in 2013 they completed a hat trick at the North Eastern Driving Trials. Tara Wilkinson, who worked for her parents breaking horses in to ride and drive, has also been training and riding/working with Boyd Exell (four-time world champion and World Cup indoor and outdoor winner) at his base in the Netherlands. International Kids Driving Event junior world gold medallist, Team GB gold medal winner in 2012, and open pony indoor champion and supreme champion in 2016, Wilkinson became the youngest driver to represent Britain the following year driving two-horse teams. She also secured an individual gold for Great Britain at the FEI World driving championships for Pony Pairs class in Minden, Germany.

'Pony pairs is combined driving,' Wilkinson explains. 'It's based a little bit around eventing. So you have the dressage, [the] marathon and then cones. The dressage is like ridden dressage; you do a dressage test. Then on the second day you do the marathon, which is basically like eventing, a long distance with speed, a little bit more technical. Then the third day is cones day ... This is basically like show jumping: you knock the ball off the cone and you get penalties ... The cones course usually has about twenty sets of cones and you have to do it within a certain amount of time.' After high school, Wilkinson went straight into working with horses; she was just sixteen. 'I started working on a Saturday when I was still in school, at a show-jumping yard ... I did that for quite a while,' she remembers. 'Then I worked for my parents, and then I started training with Boyd ... Boyd trained a lady and she needed a driver because she didn't have time what with work. So he set me up with this pony pair, which I drove for a year and a half. The second year, I drove ... and won the world championships.'

The sport is extremely technical, Wilkinson explains: 'The carriages, the horses, the bits, making sure if you drive a team or a pair. The horses have got to match, with the same head carriage, the same movement, same mindset. If you have one horse and then one quiet horse, you have to do different training, different preparation for the dressage test. You have to have a nice consistent pair of horses.' The Netherlands is considered the best country for the sport of driving, which is why Boyd Exell is based there, but it involves international travel during the season. 'The horses, the carriages, everything has to travel – the lot,' Wilkinson notes, thus making solid sponsorship imperative, given the number of European events and must-do championship courses.

Cirencester Park Polo Club

Arabella Oppenheimer Morris, Patron & player, Cirencester, Gloucestershire

(above) Arabella Oppenheimer Morris speaking to Tommy Severn, one of her Hascombe Stud team members (she is the team's patron) before mounting her pony for the finals of the Junior Cavalry Cup at Cirencester Polo Club; her mother Penny Barker looks on attentively.

Barker, who is married to Captain Fred Barker, long-time master of the Quorn Hunt in Leicestershire, is nationally recognised for her horsemanship. 'I don't ride that much these days,' she says. 'But there's nothing like riding to hounds, or the challenge of the course at Badminton'

For the quintessential English polo experience, Cirencester Park Polo Club is the supreme venue. Established in 1894 under the 7th Earl Bathurst amid 3,000 acres of parkland and woodland, Cirencester offers the highest level of polo while retaining the charm of a relaxed country setting. The club, which has a playing membership of well over a hundred, has ten match grounds, two grounds at Aston Down and a practice ground at Jackbarrow on the Miserden Estate.

Originally, just two grounds were in use for matches at Cirencester; it was not until 1909 that Lord Bathurst gave permission for the Ivy Lodge ground to be boarded. In 1933 the club was closed and its assets sold off to settle debts. Following World War I, polo was resumed in the park, with many leading players (including the then Prince of Wales) taking part in tournaments. During World War II, the Ivy Lodge ground was ploughed to grow food crops for the war effort, and it was not until 1952 that it was agreed to re-form the club now called Cirencester Park Polo Club. The present 9th Earl Bathurst remains as the Club's President, and Sundays are the traditional polo days.

Patron and player Arabella Morris Oppenheimer is the granddaughter of the late Sir Philip Oppenheimer of De Beers, and daughter of diamond dealer and racehorse owner/breeder Anthony Oppenheimer, whose horse Cracksman won Ascot in 2017. As patron of Hascombe Stud squad, Arabella has played at Cirencester, Guards, the Polo Club Saint-Tropez and the Beaufort Polo Club. Even the loss of her liver following a serious accident has not stopped her from riding, skiing and playing tennis, nor did cancer at age thirty-two. 'I have been playing at Cirencester for three years,' she notes, 'slowly progressing from two-goal tournaments to eight-goal ... I have a wonderful eight-goal team which started off winning the Badminton Cup at the Beaufort ... We have just won the Gerald Balding Victor Ludorum at Cirencester followed by the Junior Cavalry Cup ... In the winter, I went to El Remanso in Argentina, home of the Hanburys, and played the Lovelocks twelve-goal tournament with James Beim (Beimy), Captain of England, his brother Tom and Tommy Severn. Being the only female in the tournament and one of the only patrons, I felt rather brave – or mad! We had lots of injuries with both Beims going to hospital but incredibly managed to win the tournament and the wonderful prize of a Lovelocks pony for the four team members.' Oppenheimer finds male players 'stronger and bigger and more powerful' than women – 'far superior' in fact – though she clearly enjoys playing with all-female teams as well. 'I love things that are fast,' she notes. 'Getting better and going faster and getting better horses' are her goals.

Cirencester Polo Club, the oldest polo grounds in Britain, was established in 1894 and is quintessentially English. (above) The rough and tumble of polo ponies in action, with Hascombe Stud's number 3 nearly unseating the opposing team's number 3. (far left) A young groom's tattoo stands out as much as her mount as she awaits her rider's call for the mid-game quick change of ponies. (left) Eight-year-old Otto Morris dribbling the ball with his tiny polo stick, keen to participate in the real game when he comes of age. Polo is very much a family game attended by all classes; a summer's day outing with picnic hampers, wine coolers and plenty of dogs

The calm before the storm: (left) Saddles await their horses while (opposite) a set of polo sticks is spared a break or two, at least for now

The Shire Horse

Billy Sheen, Carriage driver, Howe Green, Essex

The Shire, an all-British breed, was effectively engineered in the 1840s by Robert Bakewell, who crossbred German, Flemish and Friesian horses with local breeds, especially the Old English Black. Sturdy draught animals that can weigh a ton or more, Shire stallions stand up to 18 hands. All have broad chests, thick necks and legs developed to pull up to twice the animals' own weights. Though a pair of Shires at a British exhibition in 1924 is reputed to have pulled

45 tons, Mammoth, born in 1848, is still the world's largest known horse, standing at 21½ hands and weighing 1.5 tons. At 19 hands, Goliath, a Shire gelding who died in 2001, is the world's tallest recorded horse.

Considered to be one of the main 'gins' (engines) driving the Agricultural Revolution in Britain, the Shire was used for everything from ploughing to shelling corn, working the docks, pulling pit wagons from mines to distribution centres, hauling freight on roads and canals, and turning sawmills and running the driveshafts and belts that helped launch the Industrial Revolution in the mid-nineteenth century. With the advance of mechanisation, the Shire lost the purpose for which it had been created and was relegated to drawing brewery carts and performing merely ceremonial duties. Usually black, bay or grey (mares can also be roan), the Shire is listed as at risk of extinction; Scottish Clydesdales, a Shire crossbreed, are also classified as vulnerable. Interest in the breed was revived in the 1970s, with breed societies established in Britain and other countries, culminating in the first World Shire Horse Congress in 1996. The National Shire Horse Show, held each spring in Britain, is the largest event of its kind.

Former London cabbie Billy Sheen has been a Shire enthusiast since beginning his work life driving drays at Whitbread Brewery. Asked about hansom cabs, the horse-drawn predecessors of London's taxis, Sheen says, 'It was a very, very hard life, yes it was … It wasn't a very nice life for horses, I don't think, in those times, because they were literally up in the morning, fed, out, fed on the route while the guy had his cup of tea or whatever at the cab station … and then away they went again.' During his time driving taxis, Sheen kept two Shires in stabling under the arches across from his council flat in Stepney, exercising them daily on the communal grass patch, much to the consternation of his neighbours. He remembers collecting the horses' manure and taking it to allotmenteers to use on their plots, sometimes in exchange for a bit of veg. What he misses most from that time is the feeling of community: 'We all helped each other, and the main thing we had, we had a piece of grass in the flats, and we used to take the horses on there to exercise them … A lot of the stuff we used to use then was just made-up stuff for exercising. If you had decent stuff, you would never take it out on the road; you only kept that for when you went to shows and places like Regent's Park when it was the Easter Parade.' Sheen still takes horses to county shows. 'If [the Shire] does disappear – hopefully it doesn't,' he says. 'A lot of people are getting into riding Shires now, which is keeping the breed going, keeping the breeders breeding for that purpose, but who knows what will happen in the future.'

(above) Viscount, a thirteen-year-old grey Shire stallion, at rest in the field of his owner Billy Sheen's Howe Green Farm in Essex. This splendid example of massive horseflesh stands 18 hands tall and weighed more than 2,000 pounds at the last count, eating a bale of straw and hay plus two very large buckets of feed twice a day, every day. 'He'll eat me out of house and feed, he will,' Sheen jokes. 'In the end, it's all about passion, isn't it?' (opposite) Despite its massive size, the Shire is a thing of beauty to many horse lovers. For nearly a century, Shires, Suffolk Punches and Clydesdales were the 'gin' (engines) of the British Agricultural and Industrial revolutions. Today, the Suffolk is on the 'critical' watch list, the Clydesdale is classified as 'vulnerable', and the Shire horse is listed as at risk of extinction

Royal Ascot
Ascot, Berkshire

Located about 7 miles from Windsor Castle, Ascot Racecourse is used for thoroughbred racing, hosting up to thirteen of Britain's thirty-six annual Group 1 races. Owned by Ascot Racecourse Ltd, the course has always had close links to the royal family, having been founded by Queen Anne in 1711, when, out riding, she pronounced the area of heathland 'perfect for horses to gallop'.

The inaugural event at Ascot was Her Majesty's Plate, worth 100 guineas and open to any horse, mare or gelding over six years of age. The seven runners were all English hunters, rather different from the speedy thoroughbreds that race on the flat today. The course's original length was about 6.5 kilometres. Queen Anne's role is marked by the opening of the Royal Meeting, also known as Royal Ascot, with the Queen Anne Stakes. Designed by William Lowen together with a carpenter, a painter and a racing administrator, the course was designated as public in perpetuity by an 1813 Act of Parliament, at which point the Ascot Authority was set up to manage it. Steeplechases, hurdles and other races were introduced later. The course hosts twenty-six races annually, with eighteen flat meetings held between May and October. The most prestigious event, the King George VI and Queen Elizabeth Stakes, happens each July. In 2011, Ascot celebrated its tercentenary and staged the inaugural QIPCO British Champions Day, now the climax to the European flat racing season.

Royal Ascot, held each June, has as its highlight the Gold Cup, which was first introduced in 1807. The arrival of the royal family in carriages for a procession before each race usually attracts more media coverage than the actual racing. On average, three hundred thousand people visit Royal Ascot, making it Europe's best-attended race meeting. Access to the three enclosures is restricted, and new members must apply to the Royal Enclosure Office and be invited by someone who has attended for the previous four years. The Queen herself presents both the Gold Cup and the Diamond Jubilee Stakes. In 2016, total prize money across the five days of Royal Ascot was £6,580,000.

(above) An attendee in colourful finery ready to shine at Ascot, Britain's most renowned social race meeting. (opposite) HM The Queen, accompanied by Prince Philip and their companions, arrives from Windsor Castle in 2017, a tradition dating back to 1911, when the Ascot summer race became a royal week. Founded by Queen Anne in 1711, the royal procession begins each day of Ascot, with family members arriving in horse-drawn landaus

(opposite) Contrasts in colour, style and panache among attendees in the Winners Enclosure, accentuated in recent years (right) by London's cosmopolitan élites. Ascot is the country's most popular race meeting, hosting up to three hundred thousand visitors across the five days and viewed by television audiences in more than two hundred countries

Lord Patrick Beresford

Vice-President, Guards Polo Club, Windsor, Berkshire

Lord Patrick Beresford is the brother of the 8th Marquis of Waterford, Lord Charles Beresford, whose successful polo career included winning the Gold Cup (1966, 1969) together with Patrick in a lineup that included Gonzalo Tanoira and HRH The Duke of Edinburgh. The family has been influential in polo since the nineteenth century. Lord Patrick began his service in the Royal Horse Guards in 1952, including deployments to Cyprus and as part of the British Army of the Rhine. In 1963 he transferred to No 1 (Guards) Independent Parachute Company, going on to join R Squadron of 22nd Special Air Service regiment as part of deployments to the Middle and Far East. He remains active in the veterans' community.

Guards Polo Club is one of four clubs in the UK that stages high goal tournaments. Lord Beresford became Polo Manager when Guards Polo was first opened by HM The Queen at Windsor. The two original fields would later be known as the Queen's Ground and the Duke's Ground. Then a lieutenant in the Household Cavalry, Lord Beresford was given the job of overseeing the work of the grounds. The Household Brigade Polo Club was born in 1955, with HRH The Duke of Edinburgh as President. Prince Philip had started playing while serving in the Royal Navy, where he was introduced to the sport by his uncle, Admiral Lord Mountbatten.

Lord Beresford, who was brought up in Ireland, rode from earliest childhood. 'During the war years, there was very strict petrol rationing in Ireland, so we had to go everywhere by pony and trap, if not by bicycle,' he remembers. 'So I was always with horses, loved riding, and hunting became part of my life.' Although polo is regarded by many as an élite game, he points out that it cost him nothing to play: 'I rode better than most people, and therefore I was always mounted on other people's ponies.' He began playing immediately after he left Sandhurst, later striking up a friendship with Archie David, who owned a string of polo ponies: 'He had me in his team, and I rode his ponies until he died in 1972.' Although he regards himself first and foremost as a military man, Lord Beresford was involved in equestrian sports throughout his career.

Sponsorship is critical to keeping the sport healthy. 'It helps a great deal that Her Majesty the Queen and Prince Philip are patrons,' Lord Beresford notes. 'Sponsors get a wonderful deal. They get Windsor Great Park – a wonderful setting, very convenient to London – top polo, and are pretty well guaranteed Her Majesty presenting the cup on at least three or four occasions a year.' The two forms of sponsorship include patronage – 'each of the top teams has a patron who is probably not a very good player but likes playing with professionals at a higher level' – and sponsorship – 'generally for individual tournaments, where the sponsor company puts in considerable amounts of money'.

Today, Argentina's players are far and away the best internationally. 'I would guess that the fifth-best team you could get out of Argentina would still above and beyond defeat the rest of the world,' says Lord Beresford. 'It is like a national game in Argentina. Most of Argentina is very flat, ideal for polo fields, and for centuries they've had Criollo ponies working the cattle, and from them developed polo ponies. The climate, environment – everything in Argentina is ideal for polo. And everyone plays, even children in the *estancias*.'

As to the future, Lord Beresford observes that 'there are now more polo clubs and players and ponies in England that there ever have been in history. We have suffered a blow recently – I don't want to go too deeply into this, but the Home Office has limited visas, which has affected the polo community so that it is very difficult for an Argentine player of less than a five-goal handicap, or Argentine grooms, or vets, to get visas to come to England. It hasn't affected the high goal teams so much, but it has affected the grassroots of polo. I gather that a number of players have consequentially given up.' Another challenge is the difficulty of televising matches: 'You need so many cameras and it's such a large field, a very small ball, that if you focus on the ball you don't know why people are going this way or that way. If you focus on the field, it's very difficult to see where the ball is.' Much of the sport's excitement derives from its potential for violence, 'riding an opponent off and that kind of thing. It is a contact sport, definitely. Contact between two animals weighing half a ton each … The military always like to say that polo was a good education because it taught you team spirit and it helped your riding and so on. But I think that was really just an excuse to play polo.'

(opposite) Lord Patrick Beresford against a background of wheat fields abutting his home near Hungerford, Berkshire

Guards Polo Club
Windsor Great Park, Berkshire

The origins of polo, the world's oldest team sport, can be traced back to ancient Persia. The modern game had its beginnings in India, where the Calcutta Polo Club was established by two British soldiers; élite polo spread to Britain in the 1860s, becoming an Olympic sport in the early 1900s. Two teams of four players compete on a stretch of grass 300 by 160 yards, with each chukka (round of play) lasting seven minutes. A match can be four, six or eight chukkas. A fit horse should never play two chukkas in sequence or more than two chukkas on the same day.

Guards Polo Club is one of four clubs in the UK that stage high goal tournaments. Since its establishment in 1995, it has grown to become one of Europe's largest, most prestigious clubs. In 2009, HM The Queen and HRH The Duke of Edinburgh commissioned a new royal box and clubhouse to cater to the growing membership. Three years later, there were more than a thousand non-playing members and 160 players, of whom 25 per cent were based overseas. All players pay extremely high fees, except for British Army Household Division regiments who hold the Queen's commission. The club's most prestigious annual event is the Hurlingham Polo Association's International Day (formerly Cartier International), which attracts up to thirty thousand visitors. Other events include the Queen's Cup (high goal), Royal Windsor (medium goal) and Archie David (low goal), all of which take place in June. The club also supports young polo players worldwide.

Polo is a fast, often dangerous game. The rules are designed for the safety of both the players and their ponies, whose average height is between 15 and 16 hands. Most of the best ponies come from Argentina, though they are now bred throughout the world. A good polo pony must be able to stop and turn 'on a sixpence', and most players consider that their success is largely due to the ability of their mounts. In high goal matches, many players change their horses at every chukka and can thus have several ponies each for a full match. The annual cost to patrons (who usually ride as team captains) can be as much as £10 million, while superstar plays such as the Argentinians Adolfo Cambiaso and Facundo Pieres tour the international circuit, earning upwards of £1 million a year for playing on a team as well as endorsements and display tournaments.

The English love of pageantry is as authentic and deep-rooted as the passion for tea and admiration for HM The Queen, seen here (opposite) at the presentation ceremonies for the Queen's Cup. The British fondness for irony and humour is apparent when the English and Scottish polo teams play against each other on penny-farthings (right), set off by the ceremonial uniforms of the Royal Light Cavalry (far right), whose stables are situated on Flemish Farm in Windsor

Charlie Hanbury

Professional polo player & patron, Lovelocks Polo Stud, Gloucestershire

Born in 1986, Charlie Hanbury spends six months of the year in Hungerford and the rest of his time in Lobos, Argentina. When in England, he is based at Cirencester and plays there and at Guards, Cowdray and Longdole. 'It's amazing how fast and agile such a big animal can be,' he observes of his mounts. 'There is a special bond between polo ponies and their players.'

Hanbury's father Major Christopher Hanbury, formerly Queen's Royal Irish Hussars, introduced him to polo at a young age. 'I started to ride as a child and played English pony-club polo,' says Charlie. 'My first tournament I was fourteen; I played The Associates tournament with my father at Cirencester Park Polo Club.' Currently ranked one of the UK's most successful players, he won the Cartier Queen's Cup in 2009. Other successes followed, and in 2014 he again won the Cartier Queen's Cup with his team. 2016 was the first year he played with James Beim, James Harper and Ollie Cudmore as the all-British foursome known as El Remanso. In Argentina he won four out of five tournaments, including the Copa Diamante, the Copa Guillermo Sojo and the Copa El Remanso.

'A polo horse needs to be agile, fast and able to stop in a second,' Hanbury explains, adding that the ideal pony 'is comfortable to ride and gives 110 per cent every time you play it. You need to have confidence in the horse you're riding and you will play better'. Ponies must also enjoy competing with other horses and riders. In England, Hanbury has fourteen horses in work, ten of which only play high goal while the other four play medium goal and are used as backups in case of injury. Bringing a couple of new horses into one's string each season makes a big difference to the quality of play, he believes. 'Polo is a very fast game where a lack of concentration can lose you a game as well as making it dangerous,' he notes. 'If you think that you have yourself and seven other players as well as two umpires on the field, all riding animals that weigh half a ton and go 40 miles per hour, you need to be concentrated.'

Together with his parents, Hanbury manages a breeding programme in Gloucestershire as well as at Lovelocks Polo Stud in Lobos, breeding ten and fifty fillies respectively. Rotating mounts in and out of a string 'makes a big difference', he points out. 'You have to bring them in at the top and drop the bottom ones out. That is the only way you can improve your string.' He attributes El Remanso's success to a personal trainer who helped the team enhance their performance: 'We were fit and stronger, and also changed all our diets ... and then we all invested in more horses, which made a huge difference.'

(opposite left) Fast friends and fellow patrons, international polo players Charlie Hanbury (red cap) and Charlie Wooldridge after a hard game at Guards Polo Club, showing off their newly minted trophy sons. The roughness of polo matches is apparent from the numerous sticks (opposite right) that are used and abused during each one. Hanbury (right) warming up for battle at the start of a match, dressed as a polo warrior with the face mask protecting an injury received playing a previous tournament

(above) Hanbury (number 2) and Wooldridge, along with fellow players Oliver Cudmore and Chris Hyde, lining up before the start of a match, in which Hanbury (opposite) sees animated action. Polo is a dangerous contact sport, and players are often seriously injured

(above & opposite) Only the English, one might say, mix royal pageantry, Shetland ponies and donkeys together in one continuous, eccentric display of old and new. The extraordinary diversity in carriage driving is on display post-match, organised by the British Driving Society, set up in 1957

Lila Pearson

Vice-President, Cowdray Park Polo Club, Ambersham, West Sussex

Originally from Denmark, Lila Pearson is the wife of Lord Cowdray's younger brother, Charles Pearson. A self-confessed adrenalin junkie, lover of fast cars and professional polo player, she loves the game but says, 'The horses always come first.' One of the first woman polo players, Pearson supports women in the sport but champions inclusivity rather than separate opens. Her team, Cowdray Vikings (she is their patron), won the British Ladies Polo Championships in 2016. She has her own stud combining British thoroughbreds with Argentinian breeds, as well as (unusually) her own polo training grounds.

The present Lord Cowdray invested, together with English Heritage, in stabilising the ruins on the family's estate about ten years ago so that they could be opened to the public as a romantic backdrop to the polo. The family live in Cowdray House, originally part of a gamekeeper's lodge that was enlarged in the Victorian period. The property has centuries of association with horses, starting in the Tudor period when kings and queens making their royal progress in the summer were accompanied by huge processions of horses transporting their luggage and personal effects. Visiting significant country homes along the way, the royal parties would hunt deer in the owners' forests as a prelude to feasting and drinking. The whole of the summer months was taken up by these vast progresses.

Pearson was riding before she could walk. 'My father was as obsessed with horses as I am,' she explains. 'He used to take me to see horses, to sit on them … I used to do dressage and show jumping and showing horses [but] I only started playing polo when I married my husband … I rode anything I could ride, whether it was a cow or anything else … But it wasn't just the riding. I love horses. They're my shrink, if you like. If ever I'm feeling slightly down, all I have to do is come to the stables and be with a horse and I'm all right again.' She does not think of polo as being especially perilous, observing that it is 'certainly not as dangerous as fox hunting or eventing. Yes, people have accidents, some have bad accidents, but overall when you think about how many people are playing or involved, I don't think – touch wood – that it's that bad'. At the moment, she notes, 'women are less represented [in the world of polo] than men, but every year there are more and more women playing … It's very much on the up.' Pearson does not believe that the expense of playing necessarily puts aspiring participants off. 'As a top player, you have to have at least twelve ponies when you are playing a season of polo,' she notes. 'I would say probably twenty per person, in case they go lame. You rotate them … You would have at least three grooms to look after twenty horses … The big high goal organisations have everything in house, although they're not supposed to have their own vet; it has to be overseen by an English vet. But they will have people with veterinary experience in house. They have their own farriers, everything.'

Pearson is quite certain that she could not live without having access to horses. As to personal fame, she jokes that 'people think that I was pretty okay for where I was at. I mean, I'm a patron and I'm a woman. I was the first woman to get to the semi-finals of the Gold Cup. I think people think that I do my job well enough. I do contribute to my team, as opposed to just walking!'

(opposite) Lila Pearson taking a break in her stable yard on the Cowdray Estate. 'They're my shrinks,' Pearson muses, referring to her many equine charges, one of which is being prepared for her to ride (left) on her daily afternoon canter across the estate's unending acreage

(opposite) Pearson leading
at a gallop, chasing the ball
in a friendly polo match.
Pearson (above) and her
son George, a keen polo
enthusiast since a young
age, kitting up for a match.
'There are very few patrons
that will pay for a team and
then not play themselves,'
she explains. 'Some might
put somebody younger,
stronger and better in when
they think it matters, so they
can play on the big day.'

(opposite) Edward Hitchman, principal high-goal player for Lila Pearson's Vikings team, returning from a match past the dramatic ruins of Cowdray House, a Tudor manor built in the sixteenth century. Destroyed by fire in 1793, it was once one of Britain's largest estates; the King himself hunted and feasted there. (above) A summer afternoon at Manor Farm, where the original sixteenth-century stables are located

Lila Pearson taking a break among the magnificent fields and gardens that surround her West Sussex home (right)

Greg Glue

Founder, Polo Splice, Midhurst, West Sussex

Established in 1989, Polo Splice is the UK's only mallet manufacturing company. Using the best cane from Southeast Asia and Argentine tipa wood, the company produces mallets in a range of sizes and weights, and also sells saddles, helmets and other equipment.

Greg Glue describes his profession as 'unique'. Asked whether there is a living to be made out of polo sticks, he replies, 'Yes, as long as the market doesn't get flooded with imports.' Glue, who used to play himself, became frustrated when he took his own stick to be repaired only to discover, a year later, that it had not even been taken out of the box. To remain profitable, he says, 'We need to do several thousand sticks a year, at least; five, six, seven thousand repairs per annum; and then we need to sell fifteen hundred, eighteen hundred, two thousand new sticks.'

There's no typical lifespan for a polo stick, Glue explains: 'It can last two chukkas, two games, two months ... A lot of the professionals have thirty, forty, fifty sticks, and they just rotate them.' Sticks are not tailor-made, and a particular choice is down to personal preference. 'If you're doing fifty sticks for a top Argentine or English player,' Glue adds, 'it's going to take you five hundred, maybe a thousand canes to find fifty that he might like.'

Glue travels to Malaysia and Indonesia to select his raw materials, avoiding middlemen where he can. 'There's a [supply] chain,' he explains. 'It's going to be three or four people before I get to it.' Of his own involvement with the sport, he observes, 'Everybody tries to be one of those guys that makes it through to the top, but I just couldn't get there. So I went the other way ... I saw that this was a market; we could make some money.' The appeal of the lifestyle has to do with being out of the mainstream: 'If you're a sportsman, it's not like you go to work every day, 9.00 to 5.00 ... If you can get twenty, thirty, forty sticks to one of the top players, people see that and ask, "What sticks are you using this year?" "I'm using Polo Splice sticks." "They're pretty good; let me have a feel." Then somebody else says, "I saw some sticks somebody was using the other day; can you make me twenty like that?"' For Greg Glue, word of mouth is critical to success.

Greg Glue (right), founder
of Polo Splice, displays polo
sticks made by hand at
his workshop in Midhurst
(opposite). The journey of
the not-so-humble polo
stick begins in the heart
of the jungles of Malaysia,
where the manau cane
(a woody version of bamboo)
is harvested and sold down
a long line of intermediaries
before arriving in the
capable hands of master
craftsmen

Cowdray Park Polo Club

Ambersham, West Sussex

Even the unpredictable English summer weather (above) cannot keep polo enthusiasts indoors. Cowdray Park Polo Club horses are readied for the semi-finals of the Jaeger-LeCoultre Gold Cup 2017 (opposite). Each team has its own livery and brand. The Habtoor team (shown here) is led by Dubai businessman and patron Mohammed Al Habtoor. Polo ponies are flown from one location to the other in great luxury

Cowdray Polo Park Club is set in a 16,000-acre estate owned by the 4th Viscount Cowdray. In 1588, the 1st Viscount was sequestered at Cowdray due to his Catholic beliefs; he was released in 1591 when Queen Elizabeth I visited the property. The 3rd Viscount, John Churchill Pearson, is seen as the saviour of British polo post-1945, due to the fact that he re-established a sport that had languished in Britain while becoming popular in Argentina, Australia, the US and Chile. Having a dozen ponies spare in the wake of World War II, he began training them to be leading polo ponies while practising the sport himself despite a war injury, asking his gun makers to craft an artificial arm at Roehampton Limb-fitting Centre so he could hold the reins. Pearson invited royalty and international stars to view his new team. When the Argentines Juan Nelson and Lewis Lacey visited in 1948, they were so impressed that Pearson was invited to compete in Buenos Aires the following year. The visit proved a huge success and marked a resurgence in British polo. HRH The Duke of Edinburgh became a key supporter during the early 1950s. Forming the Windsor Park team at Cowdray, he went on to establish Guards Polo Club nearer to Windsor Castle.

Influenced by Prince Philip's move to host major international competitions, Cowdray hosted the Coronation Cup in 1953. Three years later, the high goal tournament, the Cowdray Park Gold Cup, was introduced. Since then, Cowdray has grown to become one of the most prominent homes of British polo, hosting 450 games a year during the season, which lasts from April to September. The Gold Cup is sponsored by Jaeger-LeCoultre. Often referred to as the British Open, it is ranked alongside the Argentine and US open tournaments. Played during July, it lasts for four weeks with up to forty matches. The Pony Club National Championships, sponsored by Major Christopher and Bridget Hanbury, provide a springboard for youngsters, who camp out on the estate and play in a multi-age-group festival over several days.

(above) Will Harper (in blue shirt), one of the youngest professional players on the international circuit, seen in dramatic action at Cowdray Polo Club, while (opposite) Fecundo Pieres (in white shirt), one of the top five players in the world with a 10-goal handicap, shows how aggressively dangerous the game can be, as horses clash with riders and against each other in order to gain advantage over the ball

Nature to all things fix'd the Limits fit,
And wisely curb'd proud Man's pretending Wit:
As on the Land while here the Ocean gains,
In other Parts it leaves wide sandy Plains;
Thus in the Soul while Memory prevails,
The solid Pow'r of Understanding fails;
Where Beams of warm Imagination play,
The Memory's soft Figures melt away ...

When first that Sun too powerful Beams displays,
It draws up Vapours which obscure its Rays;
But ev'n those Clouds at last adorn its Way,
Reflect new Glories, and augment the Day ...

In Youth alone its empty Praise we boast,
But soon the Short-liv'd Vanity is lost!
Like some fair Flow'r the early Spring supplies,
That gaily Blooms, but ev'n in blooming Dies ...

Some Beauties yet, no Precepts can declare,
For there's a Happiness as well as Care ...

Thus Pegasus, a nearer way to take,
May boldly deviate from the common Track.

Alexander Pope, 'An Essay on Criticism'

(right) Early summer sun
makes magic of a roadside
encounter in the Cotswolds,
off the beaten track

The All England Jumping Course, Hickstead

Haywards Heath, West Sussex

(left) An afternoon of competition at the All England Jumping Course at Hickstead. The Longines Royal International Horse Show, one of the country's biggest outdoor shows, combines show jumping, showing horses and eventing. Hosted since 1992 under the patronage of HM The Queen, it has run since 1909

The All England Jumping Course at Hickstead in Sussex was designed by Douglas Bunn in 1960. Still family-run, the showground is one of the world's premier equestrian venues; almost every great show jumper has competed there. Siblings Edward and Lizzie Bunn run the showground; John Bunn is in charge of the All England Polo Club at Hickstead; and international show jumper Chloe Bunn (together with her husband and fellow show jumper Shane Breen) runs Breen Equestrian.

Douglas Bunn's ambition was to create a site that would put Britain in the same equestrian league as continental Europe and the US. Bunn also created the popular sport of team-chasing as well as the Amlin Plus Eventing Grand Prix, in which show jumpers and eventers compete against each other. Michael Clayton (former Editor of *Horse and Hound*) described Bunn as 'undoubtedly the greatest innovator in British show jumping in the post-war years ... Douglas had flair as well as originality ... He relished controversy, and was never afraid to break new ground'. Winner William Whitaker notes that 'Hickstead is a great place to bring on a young horse; there are so many classes and rings to choose from, you can bring a horse here and it'll gain more experience in a week than it would in months of competing at one-day shows elsewhere.'

Hickstead holds multiple world and European championships annually. In 2008, the course won the right to continue hosting the only FEI Nations Cup competition

in Britain. Shows in the calendar include the All England Jumping Championships, which offers the opportunity to amateur or future stars of the show-jumping world. The Al Shira'aa Hickstead Derby Meeting was founded by Bunn in 1960. Famous names who have won the class include Nick Skelton, Michael Whitaker and Harvey Smith, while Irish rider Eddie Macken holds the record for four consecutive wins. There are also dozens of showing classes, including the final of the Tattersalls RoR Show Series and Elite Performance Series. The Longines Royal International Horse Show, one of the country's biggest outdoor shows, combines show jumping, showing horses and eventing. Hosted since 1992 under the patronage of HM The Queen, it has run since 1909 and is one of the world's oldest shows. Most prestigious is the Queen Elizabeth II Cup, while the Longines King George V Gold Cup is the oldest and most significant class in the world. Finally, the Hurstpierpoint College National Schools and Pony Club Championships, held since 1964, have hosted many new international riders, among them Pippa Funnell and Robert Whitaker. The Duchess of York and supermodel Jodie Kidd both rode at Hickstead as young eventers. The course has some famous quirks, among them the Devil's Dyke, which is based on a local tourist attraction: a valley in the South Downs resembling a canyon. A colony of great crested newts who like to set up home in the water jump are annually moved out of harm's way by the local amphibian society.

Eleven-year-old Ella Willshaw (far left) looking rather chuffed at winning her first rosette while riding her horse Dulton Serenity. Hickstead, the centre of British and international horse competitions since 1960, is a major attraction for all horse enthusiasts, supporters and families from the youngest to the not so (above). A rider's splendid mane (left) competes with that of her horse as they rest before competing

Jessie Drea

Show jumper, Haywards Heath, West Sussex

Jessie Drea left school at thirteen. 'I'm actually quite academic,' she says, 'but I was bullied because I was shy, a bit of a weirdo.' She went to Hickstead for the first time at the age of three to compete in the Longines Royal International Horse Show, and has been competing ever since. Competing 'doesn't end', she explains. 'Half the battle is keeping our horses sound … keeping them from going lame. They have to jump big jumps and they are heavy … about a ton … Their ankles are no bigger than ours, and they're landing on that … Through selective breeding we've managed to breed creatures that are so strong, so athletic, but we aren't breeding joints that can take any more of the power that we're putting into them.'

Drea was fifteen when she first went to the World Championships as a member of Team GB, having been chosen by a chef d'équipe who watched her work throughout the year. 'The World Championships are every four years, like the Olympics, so I have to be careful with my horse … that I don't overuse him. By next August, which is when the World Championships are, I need him to peak,' she says. Champions are bought and sold for a wide range of prices, depending on form, fitness and their histories as jumpers. 'If someone wanted to buy my horse today, they'd have to give me two million,' Drea adds. 'If he went to the World Championships next year or was successful up until then, I could ask four or five. It's purely down to his record, his soundness and how he is in that precise moment … I wouldn't just sell him to anybody. I'd live in a gutter and have nothing before I'd sell that horse to someone who I didn't think was worthy of him.'

Between herself and her father (a breeder and trader), Drea has about fifty horses. 'We don't breed to earn money on a quick turnover anymore; we only try to breed top show jumpers.' Breeding in many ways is like gambling, and buyers come from around the world. 'If someone has the money and wants to give me it for my horse, I can't say no, which effectively will stop me getting to the peak of my sport. But it also allows me to earn a living. So it's being able to mix it right and being able to keep one horse as your shop window while selling the others.' Parting with animals she has worked with can be emotionally unsettling 'because these aren't just animals … You have to have so much trust and faith in an animal to do what we want them to do. If you walk the course at Hickstead, it's huge, and then you ride in on a horse and expect it to do it for you … I have the same affection for horses as I do with people: I love them for who they are. I love their souls.'

The demands of work and family can be overwhelming. 'I can't quit,' Drea says, 'because it's all I am … I'm under so much pressure, it's unbelievable … But there's not one day where I think, I don't want to ride today, I can't be bothered. Because the animals are still standing out there. They need me.'

(opposite) Jessie Drea at her family home and horse farm near Haywards Heath, the original buildings of which date back to the seventeenth century. Her stable (above) and tack room (right) are adorned with horsey paraphernalia. 'I sometimes call it Hell House,' Drea jokes, 'because I'm working there so much it feels like a prison – not that anyone's put me there apart from myself'

(left) Horseflesh has throughout history been judged on form, strength, stamina and character. Here Drea shows off Arthur, her twelve-year-old Irish thoroughbred, purchased in 2015. Jesse and Arthur have together been propelled onto Great Britain's equestrian team

(following spread) Mare and foal grazing in Dartmoor National Park in Devon, which contains the largest concentration of Bronze Age remains in the UK, suggesting a once-strong resident population of humans and horses. Today Dartmoor ponies range freely without human interference

Joyce & Jacky Newbery
Dartmoor pony breeders, Exeter, Devon

Joyce Newbery started showing horses when she was just seven years old. In 1972, she opened Oaklands Riding School, the largest such school in the south of England, with up to fifty horses. Twelve years later, she began showing and breeding Dartmoor ponies. Native to the UK, semi-feral ponies have roamed free on Dartmoor since the Middle Ages, and are owned and protected by Dartmoor commoners. Having been used as working animals by tin miners and quarry workers, their numbers have declined, possibly because it became illegal for a pony not to have a passport. They have small heads, large eyes, necks of medium length, muscular bodies and large chests. Jacky, Joyce's daughter, notes that 'in the 1960s, there was something like thirty thousand wild ponies on the moor; now there are about a thousand,' attesting to the steady decline in the population.

'What we breed are purebred Dartmoor ponies, which are on the list of endangered species, because the Dartmoors ... have no pedigrees,' explains Joyce. 'The ones we have have generations of pedigrees, and they are the important ones to keep the bloodlines going ... We love their attitude to everything, to breeding, to riding, to showing ... They just do anything you want them to do.' Asked whether there is a living to be made breeding Dartmoors, she replies, 'Obviously in some parts of the horse world, you can make a lot of money, but in what we do, it's a living. It's a good living, but we do it because we love it.' Jacky notes that 'horses are addictive in whatever you do with them. You want to do it well. You enjoy doing it. We teach from the grassroots level. So we see people coming into the sport ... and enjoying a lifelong commitment to it, or a career.'

Joyce and Jacky do a lot of work with the disabled, something they find particularly rewarding. 'We had a little girl not long ago, and when they sat her on the pony, she couldn't sit up,' Joyce recalls. 'She had to lay down, but she loved touching the horse; her head was on the horse's neck, and they said that just the warmth and the feel of that pony had an effect. Within three or four weeks she was sitting up. They couldn't believe the change in that time. You never see a disabled child miserable on a pony, do you?' To which Jacky adds, 'Horses are very forgiving. They don't judge.'

(opposite) Joyce Newbery and her daughter Jacky at Cowley Bridge, which spans the River Creedy. (above) Groom and stable hand Nina Marsh taking a breather from mucking out the stables, while (right) Darcie Asprey (six) tends to her pony at Oakland Riding School

Jacky Newbery (opposite)
admiring the new crop of
Dartmoor foals. (above)
Lowman Crag, a local
landmark, stands out
against the green splendour
of early summer. Dartmoor
is populated by as many tors
(granite peaks) as ponies

The New Forest Pony
New Forest, Hampshire

The New Forest in Hampshire was designated a royal hunting ground by William the Conqueror in 1079. Its ponies are native to the UK, with the breed dating back two thousand years to the last Ice Age. To keep the breed pure, colours are restricted to chestnut or bay. Stallions are let out into the forest between April and July to breed with the mares. The so-called 'Verderer' decides which stallions are allowed to breed. Foals are born in the spring and summer; once rounded up with their mothers, they are assumed to be the property of the mares' owners. All ponies in the forest are essentially wild but owned by commoners – individuals who have lived there all their lives and have the land to hold the horses. New Forest ponies are classed as a rare breed due to the declining horse market. Calm and gentle, they are often raced locally and are quite fast, especially over rough terrain. Naturals at jumping and gymkhana, they are also successfully trained to carry handicapped riders.

Agisters are employed by the Verderers to watch over the forest to ensure that the owners of depastured stock and others meet the Verderers' standards in respect of stock welfare. They attend road accidents and other incidents involving commoners' animals, deal with injured animals and humanely destroy them if necessary. Agisters organise the construction and maintenance of stock pounds as well as arranging and managing the rounding up of ponies. When Agisters have collected marking fees from commoners, they will clip the ponies' tails to a set pattern to indicate proof of payment. Pony 'drifts' or 'roundups' are held in the summer and autumn. Herding the animals together in a pound allows several jobs to be done at once, including tail clipping and veterinary checks. Any colts are taken off the forest before they can breed, as are ponies that are to be sold or kept on a holding through the winter.

Eighteen-year-old Hayden Prince, who lives in Bramshaw, studied Equine Science at college. Her course, she says, 'basically covered everything from breeding to vetting to showing. And it's really set me up'. Prince wants to go into teaching but also is a budding polo player, so needs to juggle her schedule to accommodate both. She describes New Forest ponies' unique character this way: 'At the same time as being wild, they all have quite a kind temperament. They are easy to handle and are easily one of the kindest and beautifullest breeds ... Obviously, the ones that are in the forest, you leave in the forest. If you want to bring some off from the forest and breed them, then you can. Everything that is in the forest is owned [by somebody].'

Hayden Prince (above) with new-found friends in the New Forest. 'It's easy when you have a couple of apples in your pocket,' she says

Goodwood

Chichester, West Sussex

Set next to Trundle Iron Age hill fort, Goodwood is owned by the family of the Duke of Richmond, whose seat is nearby Goodwood House. In 1758, the 2nd Duke built the stables in which runners are still accommodated today for his hunters; the buildings were designed by the architect and founder-member of the Royal Academy Sir William Chambers. Goodwood was launched as a flat horseracing course for local officers by the 3rd Duke in 1802 when their invitation to race in nearby Petworth Park was withdrawn. The opening race, the Hunting Club Subscription, cost 20 guineas to enter and was run in 2-mile heats.

Suspended during World War II, Goodwood's popularity continued to grow after the conflict ended. In 1952, it became the first British course to provide live commentaries over loudspeakers; four years later, the first races were shown on television. Over the years the track has seen many changes, with stands being demolished and replaced. The course itself is unusually complex: straight six furlongs (there are eight furlongs in a mile), uphill and downhill. The season starts in May and ends in September. The best-attended meeting is the Qatar Goodwood Festival, popularly known as 'Glorious Goodwood'. In 2015, the total prize money on offer for Glorious Goodwood received a £2 million boost thanks to Qatar sponsorship and totalled over £4.5 million for the thoroughbred races. As Lord March, owner of the Goodwood Estate, put it, 'Qatar completely understands the significance of our rich history ... To be racing at Goodwood and know you are seeing the best horses competing for the highest prizes adds hugely to the excitement and atmosphere of the festival.'

(above) Merry punters striking poses, ever mindful of prying cameras. The extraordinary capture

(opposite) of a precious moment between a young girl and her father is telling in its silent regard, right at the moment the winning horse is displayed on the large screen behind them. One is left to wonder whether the father's inscrutable demeanour betrays a winning bet or a losing punt

(right) Grizelda Cowan (seventy-five) with her granddaughter Emma Hooley (thirteen) enjoying a blustery afternoon ride along the beach at Rudder's Point near the village of Lower Largo in Fife, Scotland

Tom Walling & Gemma Pearson

Cumbria Arabians, Over Whitlaw Farm, Selkirk, Scottish Borders

In 1996, Cumbria Arabians relocated to Over Whitlaw Farm, previously one of Scotland's most successful racing stables under trainer Bobby Fairburn. The stud had been founded twenty years earlier by Tom Walling's mother, Fiona, with two English-bred mares, Narrisa (Naidarus x Risnab) and Royal Gayza (Harwood Asif x Silver). Spotting a niche in the British market, she imported a black stallion, Mista Beaujangles, in 1980; he went on to be an important sire, especially of endurance horses. Anglo-Arabians are a cross between Arabians and thoroughbreds, with a minimum 12.5 per cent of Arabian blood. Originally bred by Bedouins for long desert treks and quick forays into enemy camps, Arabians developed a large lung capacity and incredible endurance.

'I was able to sell the black foals more or less straight after weaning from the mother,' Fiona remembers. 'That was the highest point, where you could get the most profit.' Her market was initially other breeders because the black was so rare; it was essential to run her stud as a profitable business to justify its presence on the farm. The horses would run out with the cattle (and still do today), and the mares 'out-wintered; they are very hardy ... At one stage, the stud was about twenty-five horses, but it's never been very big. This is the smallest it's been'. Tom describes the challenges of farming this way: 'Even for a young person trying to rent land, the overheads involved in getting set up, in buying your stock or your machinery, even the rent – the money involved is quite substantial ... We're very lucky because my dad and mum (and Robert Hudson, who is a business partner in the farm) have set us up in the Scottish Borders.'

Tom and Gemma met when Gemma was showing Belted Galloway cattle. 'Tom and the family had a Belted Galloway bull that they wanted to show at the Great Yorkshire Show... so through a mutual friend I showed this bull for them,' Gemma remembers. 'Tom says it was the most expensive Great Yorkshire Show he's ever been to!' Today she is a vet at the University of Edinburgh, specialising in behavioural issues. She is also Veterinary Liaison Officer for the International Society for Equitation Science. She notes that Cumbrian Arabians race over hills, mud, woodland and stony tracks, and summarises their level of fitness this way: 'From the endurance rider's point of view, you want a horse whereby if you stop to close a gate and the other horses gallop off, your horse doesn't get too upset.'

Tom Walling and Gemma Pearson (left) with some of their Black Arabian horses pasturing freely in the Eildon Hills

(opposite) An Edwin Landseer moment, as horse and cattle mingle on the grasslands of the Scottish hills. (above) Gemma Pearson out riding Beaujangles, a five-year-old Arabian stallion who is, she says, 'pure poetry ... a dream to ride, with an easy-going temperament'. This goes with the territory, one would assume from the image

Lucinda Russell OBE

Trainer, Arlary House Stables, Milnathort, Kinross, Fife

The younger of two children, Lucinda Russell began riding at two-and-a-half. She started training in 1995, having previously evented, show-jumped and trained point-to-pointers. In 2017 she trained One For Arthur, becoming only the fourth woman to train a Grand National winner (and only the second winner from Scotland). 'I'd have to look up the dates to get it exactly right, but in the 1920s there were no women trainers,' Russell notes. 'If you wanted to train a horse, you'd put it in a man's name. In my lifetime, I don't think I've seen any sexual discrimination, but it's within touching distance. I think fewer people said to me, 'Well done for winning the National because you're a woman.' I had a lot of people say to me, 'Well done for winning the National because you're from Scotland.'

Russell's day-to-day routine involves compiling work lists, liaising with head lads and assistant trainers, keeping in contact with owners and riding out. 'My family moved here when I was thirteen,' she says of her estate in Milnathort. 'It's a beautiful Georgian house, and it had a beautiful parkland with trees, and then I have built fifty stables at the bottom of their beautiful garden!' The family joke was always that when Russell was little, she wanted a pony. 'We have a holiday house down by the coast,' she says, 'and they had pony rides, and I used to lead the ponies up and down the beach, and get free rides. That's how I started: leading the beach ponies.' After attending the University of St Andrews, she started riding again, doing three-day eventing and going abroad on teams. One of the horses she trained successfully was an ex-racehorse whose owners asked her to send it point-to-pointing, and it won. 'Then I was asked to take up my licence by one of the owners.

I didn't really know that much about racing,' she adds.

Russell's partner and assistant trainer Peter Scudamore (one of the few British jockeys to have won eight championships) received an MBE for services to racing at the end of his riding career. In 2014 'Scu', who rode 1,678 winning horses in the course of his career, became a jockey coach; he now helps Russell's conditional jockeys with their riding, schooling and race tactics. On arriving at Arlary, Scu told Russell, 'If we're going to train horses, we have to train a hundred horses' – at which point they brought in more jockeys. 'Now, we have probably eighty horses ... it's really my ideal world,' Russell says. While acknowledging her privileged background, she adds, 'I've never been one to go out and buy the most expensive horse in the sale. What's important to me is the actual horse ... I've got a lot of experience of seeing them, of trying to get inside the horse's mind ... To be a racehorse, you've got to be a very special type of horse. You've got to be brave, you've got to go through the pain barrier, you've got to have a desire to be in front. If I think about the number of horses that I've ever known or owned or had through my hands, it'd be many, many thousands ... When you see One For Arthur [for example], he's very much a racehorse. He's very noble. They've got an immense strength about them. But he's a very kind horse. They're not bullies, they're not scared, they have a confidence about them. Maybe it's a bit like people. They don't necessarily have to be aggressive, the best athletes. They have to be level-headed.' Training fees only just cover her costs; the profit is in the prize money, of which Russell is entitled to only 10 per cent. That may not sound like much, but, as she says, 'Think of the joy!'

Lucinda Russell (left) alongside her partner Peter Scudamore (one of Britain's best-known jockeys), discussing strategy with one of their jockeys before a race at Perth Racecourse. (opposite) Russell with One For Arthur, the 2017 winner of the Grand National at Aintree. This was only the second time that a Scottish horse and trainer won this race-of-all-races

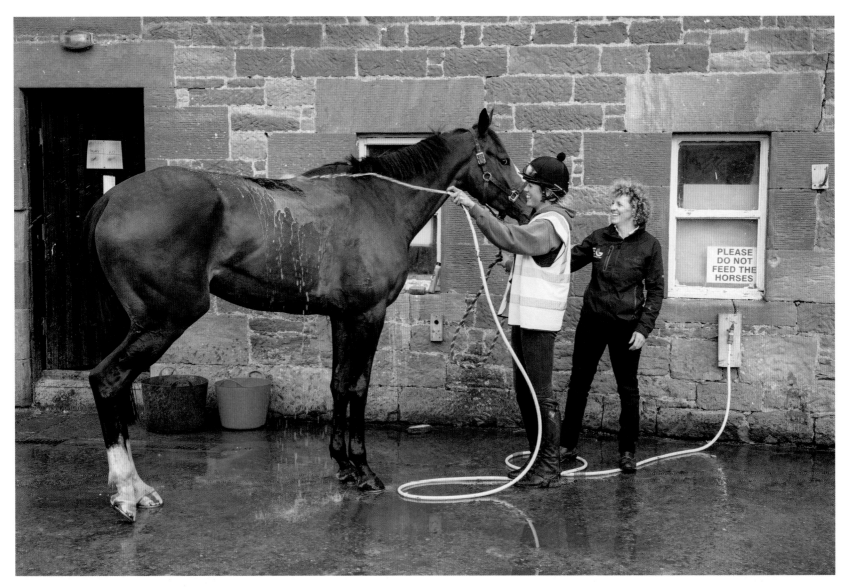

(above) Hosing down the horses at Arlary House Stables after morning gallops. (opposite) Scenes from an afternoon of racing at Perth Racecourse, including schoolgirls sporting their favoured jockeys' colours. Over £300 million was generated by racing in Scotland in 2016

PLEASE DO NOT FEED THE HORSES

Annette Noble
Clydesdale breeder, Peggyslea Farm, Penicuik, Midlothian

(left) Annette Noble with her daughter Ailsa and one of their Clydesdales at Peggyslea Farm in Midlothian. (opposite) The giant Peggyslea Andy and owner Annette heading back to the stable

Originally from Dumfries and Galloway, Annette Noble and her family live 10 miles south-west of Edinburgh at the foot of the Pentland Hills. She has stabling for up to six horses, as well as an illuminated paddock with professional riding surface (and a barn filled with classic cars). Noble has won numerous prizes with her horses, among them 2017 Clydesdale Champion, Royal Highland Show; and 2017 Gelding Champion, National Stallion Show.

You might say that Clydesdales are in Noble's blood, as both her grandfather and her father bred, showed and drove them. In fact, her father threatened to leave the family farm when his father proposed replacing their Clydesdales with machines. The tradition continues: Noble's daughter rides Clydesdales competitively (her son races cars). Originally draught horses, Clydesdales are some of the biggest horses on the circuit. Having become popular in the late nineteenth century, they were exported throughout the world, becoming known as 'the breed that built Australia' among other things. Though Clydesdales were considered vulnerable to extinction by the 1970s, Noble does not think they will ever disappear 'because there's more

people getting interested in them again ... just for a hobby. There are people making money, dealing them a bit, buying and selling them.'

Before the advent of tractors, Clydesdales 'did all the work' right across Britain though mostly in Scotland (Shire horses were favoured in England). 'Ploughing, sowing the seed, harvest – they did everything ... every farm had them,' Noble explains. 'So [they numbered in the] thousands.' Showing and riding are hardly big earners; in fact, Noble describes them as 'all hobby ... If you go to local shows you'll be lucky if you win, first prize in hand, £10. And then, at something like the Highland Show, they'll give you something like £100 for first prize'. She says of her Clydesdales that 'they tend to be good-natured horses ... They get treated to luxury now, don't they. The thing is, it's good for them. We go to the shows, there's other people around, all the competitors. It's a nice social scene as well. Obviously, we compete with each other at the shows, but afterwards we can socialise and it's really nice ... We breed them and then break them in, so they're not costing us a lot of money ... anything from £1,000 to £20,000.'

(left) Annette Noble's tack room with the Scottish flag and a Clydesdale's enormous collar. Every tack room reflects its owner's style, preferences and attention to detail, representing both horses and horse people more emblematically than any other feature of a stable complex

Francis Bakker

Equine dentist & vet, North Berwick, East Lothian

Francis Bakker is a qualified vet and equine dentist based at Sheriff Hall Farm Cottage outside of North Berwick, a seaside town that was fashionable as a holiday resort in the nineteenth century. Having studied Veterinary Medicine at Utrecht University and in the US, she established her practice on the Scottish Borders, adjusting her fees to match her clients' budgets. A member of the Association of British Veterinary Acupuncturists, Bakker regularly posts pictures of horses' teeth on her Facebook page.

'I've always ridden,' says the vet. 'My father started me in riding and competing. When I started in veterinary training, I would do all kinds of animals but ... decided to specialise in equine dentistry. Being a vet is partly to make a living and partly because I have a passion for it.' When she first came to the UK, Bakker lived in Durham, then in Cumberland and elsewhere, finally ending up in Scotland 'because the riding is phenomenal. You are allowed to ride anywhere you want. I like the Scots and the hills; you don't see enough hills in Holland'. Her passion for endurance riding originated with her move to Scotland. 'It's very addictive,' she says of the sport. 'You always want to go further and explore new areas. It creates such a bond between you and your horse. In that respect, it's a very special discipline ... Not many people get to spend hours in the middle of nowhere with just their horse.'

Bakker owns five Arab horses, which, she explains, 'are most suited for longer distances. But any horse with the right training can do it ... The horse has to be sensible but like to go. It has to have the right attitude to keep going. We only train three times per week and go over any terrain, but you don't do many miles in training. You have to have a horse that pays attention to where it's going and doesn't stumble. Horses are fitter than you think. It takes much longer for a human to train for a marathon than a horse to be ready for an endurance ride'. Bakker's ultimate goal is to participate in 'a ride in France, in Montcuq, which is a two-day ride and 125 miles in one day'; her interim goal is the Golden Horseshoe Ride, a two-day event of 100 miles over Exmoor in Devon.

Francis Bakker (above) taking a tea break before beginning work on floating a horse's teeth. (opposite) The term *floating* means to smooth or contour a horse's teeth with a file (called a float). As a horse's teeth continue to grow throughout its life, they can become sharpened from constant grazing, and therefore need to be ground down once a year, often while the horse is sedated

Constance Newbould
Endurance rider, Damhead, Midlothian

With more than forty years of experience with horses, Constance Newbould competes regularly at local club shows. At the Scottish Regional Group AHS Spring Performance and Showing Show in 2014, she was the winner of In-hand endurance horse, In-hand purebred youngstock and of In-hand purebred aged four years and over. Newbould is one of only a handful of riders in Scotland to have obtained a Diamond award, having completed 100 miles in one day.

As Managing Director at Pentland Livery Stables Ltd, Newbould runs a small, exclusive livery yard recognised for its horse welfare and customer care. She formally served as Director (Accountant) at Endurance GB, the national governing body for the sport of endurance riding. She has been appointed to over twenty different companies in the past and held her first appointment at the age of thirty-eight.

'I'm a breeder of Arabs and I took up endurance in 1997,' Newbould explains. 'My first horse that I did endurance with was half-Arab, half-Welsh Cob thoroughbred. I realised that what I needed more was an Arab, to do faster speeds. So I looked into Arabs to see what sort did the best endurance, and I decided that Crabbet Arabs from Crabbet Park were the best ... It was Lady Blunt who bred Crabbet Arabs at Crabbet Park. She imported six mares originally from the desert, and all of her horses

go from there ... I decided that was where I wanted to go, and I went and bought a hundred-per-cent Crabbet Arab, Diamond Banner. But unfortunately he got OCD in his hock so I couldn't continue. Then I bought his sister, and I didn't like her, or she didn't like me. At the same time that I bought her, I bought a Polish Arab. (I only bought the Polish Arab because I'm half Polish).' Many other top horses followed.

Newbould has done endurance riding in every kind of weather over enormous distances, which, she notes, are 'hard on everybody. It's hard mentally'. She is accompanied by support staff who provide water and a 'buffet' for horse and rider alike. There are compulsory halt points, known as vet gates, usually every 25 miles. The horse 'gets his heart rate taken, gut sounds, capillary refill, mucus membranes and gait. They trot him up and down to make sure he's sound and he's not hurt himself ... Usually there's a thirty- or forty-minute hold, then you go out again and do another 20 or 30 miles, then you have another hold ... With endurance, the longest race they do at the moment is 160 in a day at the World Equestrian Games ... For the [Longines] FEI I think you've got to have 160 minutes of hold if it's 160 kilometres'. So what drives her to compete? 'It's the bond between me and my horse,' Newbould replies. 'Kai does it because I ask him.'

(opposite) Constance Newbould tending to her pregnant Arabian mare, bred for endurance, and (right) silhouetted against a stormy Scottish sky after a hard canter on her mount Zarkhruv

The Shetland Pony

Harry Sleigh, Breeder, Fyvie, Turriff, Aberdeenshire

Harry Sleigh (above) herding his unruly Shetland stallions at Wells Shetland Pony Stud in Aberdeenshire. 'This,' Sleigh says, 'is not a life for everyone.' Too right, Harry! (opposite) Sunshine highlights a Shetland stallion's sturdy features and fierce gaze

Wells Shetland Pony Stud was founded in 1901 by John P. Sleigh at St Johns Wells, Fyvie. Under Harry Sleigh's grandfather, the stud expanded, starting in 1947, with ponies being exported to America, Australia and continental Europe. Ponies were also sold throughout the UK, providing the foundation stock for numerous studs. Many of the exported ponies won or produced champions in their new countries. The stud's first Royal Highland Show championship win was in 1950 and now stands at a total of thirty-three Royal Highland and sixteen Royal English champions.

Shetland ponies originated in the isles of the same name. Short, stocky and highly intelligent, their heavy coats protect them from the harsh climate. Due to their strength, they were used for packing in coal mines in the US as late as 1971. Harry Sleigh describes his ponies as part of 'family history [and] a passion ... It's a hobby, it's a business, it's quite a large part of our, and especially my, life'. His great-great-grandfather's involvement as a breeder began in the 1800s at Haddo House, where he was a tenant farmer. His sons 'started with Clydesdales and would have been one of the top Clydesdale breeders ... They took over St Johns Wells as a tenant farm from Haddo House in 1901, and it was one of the biggest farms in the area. Farms weren't measured in acres in those days; they were measured in pairs of horses. There were six pairs of horses at St Johns Wells ... The working horses ... did ... all the agricultural work'.

Sleigh's grandfather had five stallions which 'would have been leased out ... One groom or horse handler would go with that horse round all the farms in that area, all summer, and be paid a certain amount of money ... A number of very successful farmers became renowned for breeding excellent horses. Two or three of these people ... moved into Shetland ponies'. It was Lord Londonderry who started using them as pit ponies. At the time, 'a Shetland pony would have been allsorts. There would have been big ones, small ones; there was no recognised breeding to improve the Shetland pony ... until the late 1800s with Lord Londonderry. He revolutionised the horses.'

Sleigh's grandfather, he says, 'quickly rose to the very top of the Shetland ponies', a process he ascribes to a combination of luck and skill. 'My grandfather bought a horse from Harviestoun and it just changed the Wells stud from being good to being one of the top.' Today, the Shetland is valued as 'the strongest horse in the world bar none. It can fight its corner; it will fight a bigger horse to get what it feels it needs. It's very determined, very stubborn. It has all the characteristics of its landscape: tough, hardy, rugged [and] temperamental, a bit like the weather!'

The Highland Pony
Kingussie, Inverness-shire

(above) Highland ponies range freely on pastures with the Cairngorms in the background, and (opposite) grazing in front of Ruthven Barracks, an English garrison fort burned down by the Jacobite rebel commander Viscount 'Bonnie' Dundee (Bonnie Prince Charlie) while retreating after the defeat of his army at the Battle of Culloden (1746)

Highland ponies are native to Scotland, primarily the north. One of Britain's oldest breeds, they were never purposely cross-bred to other animals to create a type; instead, the environment shaped their unique characteristics.

Until quite recently, the breed was divided into Western Isles ponies, standing between 13 and 14 hands, and larger, heavier Highland ponies, often erroneously called garrons (a word derived from the Gaelic for 'gelding') bred on the mainland and standing from 14 to 14.2 hands. Nowadays no official distinction is made. The ponies' strength and sure-footedness assure their continued demand for carrying sportsmen up the Scottish hills and carrying stags weighing up to 16 stone (with a special saddle, itself a considerable weight) down the same rough, precipitous hills. HM the Queen has a large working stud of Highland ponies which are used during the season to carry stags, hinds and panniers.

Today the breed enjoys international popularity, and there are studs not only in Scotland but in England, Wales, Continental Europe, the US and Australia. They are very hardy and tough, rarely require shoeing and are very economical to keep. Their ability to grow fat on 'nothing but air' is similar to that of most mountain and moorland breeds because the food available naturally in their habitats is generally of poor quality and sparse on the ground. Highland ponies' calm nature and sure tread might even invite a description of the breed as 'dull', a perception enhanced by their typical 'dun' colours of grey, cream and yellow.

Louisa Milne Home

Eventer & trainer, Craigo, Kinross, Perth

Louisa Milne Home's tack room (above), adorned with colourful rosettes earned during a long eventing career

It was after graduating from the Royal Agricultural College with a BSc (Hons) in 2001 that Louisa Milne Home set up her competition yard. Since then she has produced six horses to Advanced level as well as produced and sold horses to aspiring eventers. The only Scottish rider – and one of only thirty-four British riders – to be graded category A by the International Federation for Equestrian Sports, she does not have lots of trainers but learns from watching other riders on the circuit. 'Attitude, paces, scope, conformation' are the attributes she looks for in a horse.

'I'm one of the top Scottish riders at the moment and one of the few who's been competing regularly at 4 star in Scotland for the last seven or so years ... so we've had a nice run of things for a little while,' says Milne Home. One of her main reasons for going to agricultural college was that 'we did three weeks travelling around France and Germany, looking at different stud farms and the sales in Germany ... and then we went to America for three weeks, and went to Kentucky and ... the big Godolphin yards and the big breeding sales, and trotting out ... You sometimes don't realise how many different jobs there are in the horse industry – you get stuck into your own little area – so it was amazing'. Milne Home was always 'just really keen to have ponies ... All the way through Pony Club I had a really good bunch of friends ... We were all quite competitive so we pushed each other ... I would ride out for racehorse trainers in the holidays and then event, and then before uni I ... worked for Stephen Clarke, who is a very high-powered dressage judge ... When I went to university, I didn't think that I would be an eventer as a full-time job because I didn't think that necessarily could *be* a full-time job!'

Eventing may be dangerous, but that does not worry Milne Home. 'It depends what you're sat on,' she observes. 'I've been lucky and had some really nice horses that might not have been perfect all round, but they've been good jumpers ... If you and they move up sensibly, you do believe that you can keep doing it, so as long as you're not pushing yourself beyond what you're comfortable doing ... Saying that, you do get nerves, and probably more so now that you're a bit older, about the bigger competitions!' Eventing is all-consuming, allowing little time for relationships, travelling or anything else; a rider's relationship is with the horse, the yard and the training. 'It's a little bit antisocial from that point of view!' Milne Home laughs. 'I do find it difficult to book out a weekend and say I'm going to do something different. The summer is the horses and you think, Well, I can be a little bit more relaxed in the winter.'

Milne Home (right) in the stables next to her home, fondly caressing her favourite horse, King Ida, an eighteen-year-old Belgian warmblood (now retired) who has competed in nine 4-star events, even though he is not a thoroughbred

Louisa Milne Home (left) riding her palomino Future Plans in the brilliant sunshine, overlooking Ledlanet Reservoir near Perth

Boots and hooves in competition (following spread). Local dressage riders taking a break at a pub near Haywards Heath, West Sussex, while polo ponies work out during daily practice on the Cowdray Estate, Ambersham

Izzy Taylor
Eventer, Bicester, Oxfordshire

(above) Izzy Taylor in her
stable yard with her lurcher
Ronald and a spaniel friend

Eventer Izzy Taylor is based in Oxfordshire near her family
farm and Heythrop Hunt country. Taylor began riding
when she was very young and first went hunting on a pony
at age four. The women in her family have been active in
riding and showing for generations. Her grandmother Jane
Whiteley finished second at Badminton Horse Trials; her
great-aunt Anneli Drummond Hay was an élite event rider
and show jumper; and her mother Nicola Taylor competed
in eventing at an élite level and was Master of Bicester Hunt
for many years. Izzy's father Robert has acted as Secretary
of the College Valley and North Northumberland Hunt.

Taylor rents and runs a busy yard with her partner
and fellow eventer Oli Smith. 'It's actually owned by a
building construction company,' she says of the property.
The company has already started building on the land,
and she is sad to think of leaving. 'It's a beautiful place
here,' she notes. 'I've known it for years.' Taylor turned
down university places to study sports science in order
to continue her eventing career. After spending a season
at Hartpury College working for breeders Sam and Linda
Barr, she worked with Olympic show jumper Markus Fuchs.
While based in Holland in 2003, she fractured two vertebrae
and displaced another in a fall. After spending several weeks
on her back, Taylor had lost so much weight and muscle
tone that she had to learn how to move again – including
how to walk. Three years later, she returned home to set up
her own yard alongside her mother's hunters' liveries.

'We have twenty-nine stables, and at the moment
there are probably twenty horses here,' Taylor explains.
'It fluctuates throughout the year with the hunters and
the eventers.' There are three full-time and two part-time
grooms on her staff, and her top horse is Heythrop Hunt
Secretary Guy Avis' Briarlands Matilda. Taylor is a regular
on the British team for the Nations Cup series. As an
international event rider, she is currently ranked second
in the British Eventing rankings and fourteenth in the
FEI World rankings.

(above) Serafina, an attractive mare with good athletic abilities and 'future potential' (according to Taylor), is washed down after a ride. (left) Taylor's tack room is filled with trophies and mementoes

Bucolic autumn Oxfordshire settings: (above) The long shadows of sunset's creep extend across recently ploughed fields of wheat, while horses (right) shelter from the heat

Hattie Lawrence

Clinical Director, Valley Equine Hospital, Lambourn, Berkshire

Before becoming an assistant at Valley Equine Hospital in Lambourn, Hattie Lawrence spent a year in mixed practice and ran her own ambulatory practice. Today she is responsible for the over-ground endoscopy service and takes both internal and external referrals. Her caseload is divided between horses in training and élite event horses, and she acts as a veterinary surgeon at Kempton, Sandown and Epsom. She also carries out pre-purchase examinations in the UK and overseas.

'Lambourn has about fifteen hundred horses in training, both National Hunt and flat racehorses, and, associated with that, a number of thoroughbred breeding operations,' Lawrence explains. 'The reason that Lambourn developed was that we are on beautiful chalk downland, very free-draining soil, which meant that the grassland would remain suitable for horses throughout the year.' The condition of the so-called 'ground' is important for two main reasons: 'For breeding stock, the importance is that the quality of the grass is good ... [Also] the horses don't suffer with problems with their feet and skin as a result of being in mud for prolonged periods during the winter.' Ancient horses 'ranged over vast areas, so they could move to higher, drier ground during wet weather. Secondly, horses that were genetically predisposed to getting [skin and hoof problems] would generally not survive or thrive to breed, so evolution would come into play and those horses would effectively be bred out of the population. From our point of view, we have selectively bred a population that is all about speed. So we have function interfering with evolution. That's where the veterinary side of the

management of the racehorse becomes key'. The quest for good ground is, Lawrence emphasises, 'key to successful training. Nowadays we have artificial surfaces ... generally a combination of sand and some sort of fibre or rubberised material, and increasingly the whole surface is treated with a waxy substance, which means that it produces a stable mat. So it's cushioning, but when the horse puts its foot down, there's much less slippage'. Interestingly, none of the 'classic or high-group races are run on all-weather; they're all on turf'.

Typical injuries that Lawrence faces as a surgeon include orthopaedic injuries, with fractures being relatively commonplace in racehorses due to training pressures to perform at a young age. Thoroughbred two-year-olds, for example, are bred to be both physically and emotionally feisty. Because they will have been handled from birth, they are used to human contact so are unlikely to behave like prima donnas. 'They don't give us any reason to think they aren't happy,' Lawrence notes. 'They're very keen to train ... We've created this kind of animal where this is their *raison d'être*, to gallop. Then we give them that opportunity. We are harnessing this important evolutionary response, which is if you are in a herd, and you are being pursued by a predator, the fastest one is the one that doesn't get eaten ... The jockey's whip ... that sort of reflex of the whip touching the hindquarter – is effectively replicating the idea of a predator ... You see in Africa how they reach up and grab the hindquarters. If there are other horses either side of that individual, their instinct is to run faster because that way they don't get eaten.'

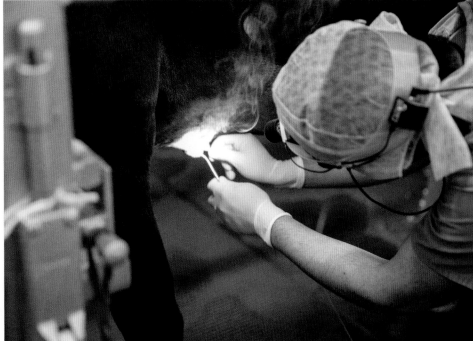

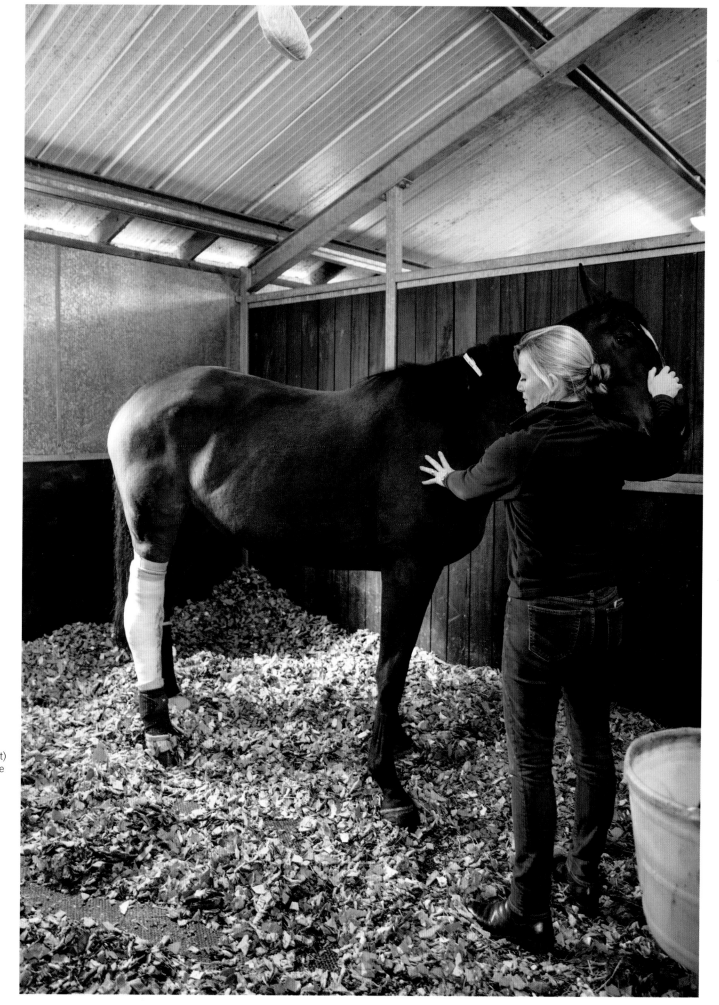

(opposite left) Hattie Lawrence taking a mobile break by the clinic's horse ambulance. (opposite right) Laser surgery on a sarcoid (a type of tumour that usually grows on a horse's underside) on an anaesthetised animal. (right) Lawrence tending to a horse just out of surgery at the clinic's stables

Oliver & Tarnya Sherwood

Trainers, Rhonehurst, Lambourn, Hungerford, Berkshire

Oliver Sherwood has ridden a total of ninety-six winners, a significant total for a non-professional, and became a champion amateur in 1979–80. In 1986, his wife Tarnya rode in the Grand National (a race Oliver himself won in 2015). Today they run a medium-sized stables complete with picturesque courtyards, manicured lawns and ornamental trees. Although Oliver admires the success of huge modern yards, he has no interest in sharing their approach.

Oliver describes Rhonehurst's weekly schedule as follows: 'Tuesdays and Saturdays are work mornings; Mondays and Fridays are routine exercise; Wednesday's quiet; Thursday's a jumping day.' The stables has sixty boxes and is home to as many racehorses. 'I like to think we're professional, and I don't like being beaten at tiddlywinks, let alone on a racehorse,' Oliver laughs. 'I'm very lucky. Compared to a lot of other yards in the area, we have a lot of turnout facilities, so the horses can go out in the paddocks for an hour, couple of hours, whatever. It does their minds good.' But racing is not all about riding. 'I think I'm right in saying it's the second most important employer of people, of sport, in the country, behind football,' he notes. 'I've got a small business. I employ fifteen, eighteen people; the farriers are self-employed. You've got the vets, stall-handlers, riders out – it goes on forever. Lambourn is a big centre of racing … I think I'm right in saying there's eight hundred, nine hundred horses in the village, twenty-five, twenty-eight trainers in the vicinity … The majority, some of them are flat trainers, some of them are jump trainers, National Hunt trainers.'

Tarnya explains that while Oliver is in charge of training, she rides out her own horses, adding, 'I am very much involved in the day-to-day running of the yard … Because I am in the string every day, three lots every day, I see things that maybe [Oliver] doesn't always see … but he himself decides how he uses that information.' She describes the sharing of specific responsibilities this way: 'We have a head lad who feeds all the horses and goes and checks all the horses morning and night. He would know every single horse inside out … Oliver and he discuss … what to do with various horses … and if some horses have gone off their food … We also have an assistant trainer; the assistant trainer again is an assistant to Oliver and to the head lad, and he tends to deal with all of the issues with staff and making sure that everyone is at work and doing the right things and that they are all happy … The whole thing is run very much as a team.' On the issue of women in sport, Tarnya notes, 'I think there are some very, very good lady jockeys riding right now, and there are some very good lady trainers. I think it helps [to have women] in the yard as well. Especially when some of these young lads and lasses are working away from home for the first time, it helps to have someone to put an arm around their shoulder from time to time and make sure they are okay … Because at the end of the day, happy staff make happy horses.'

Tarnya Sherwood (left) in action at Rhonehurst racing stables and training facilities. (opposite) Oliver Sherwood calming one of the younger horses in another part of the stables in preparation for a ride

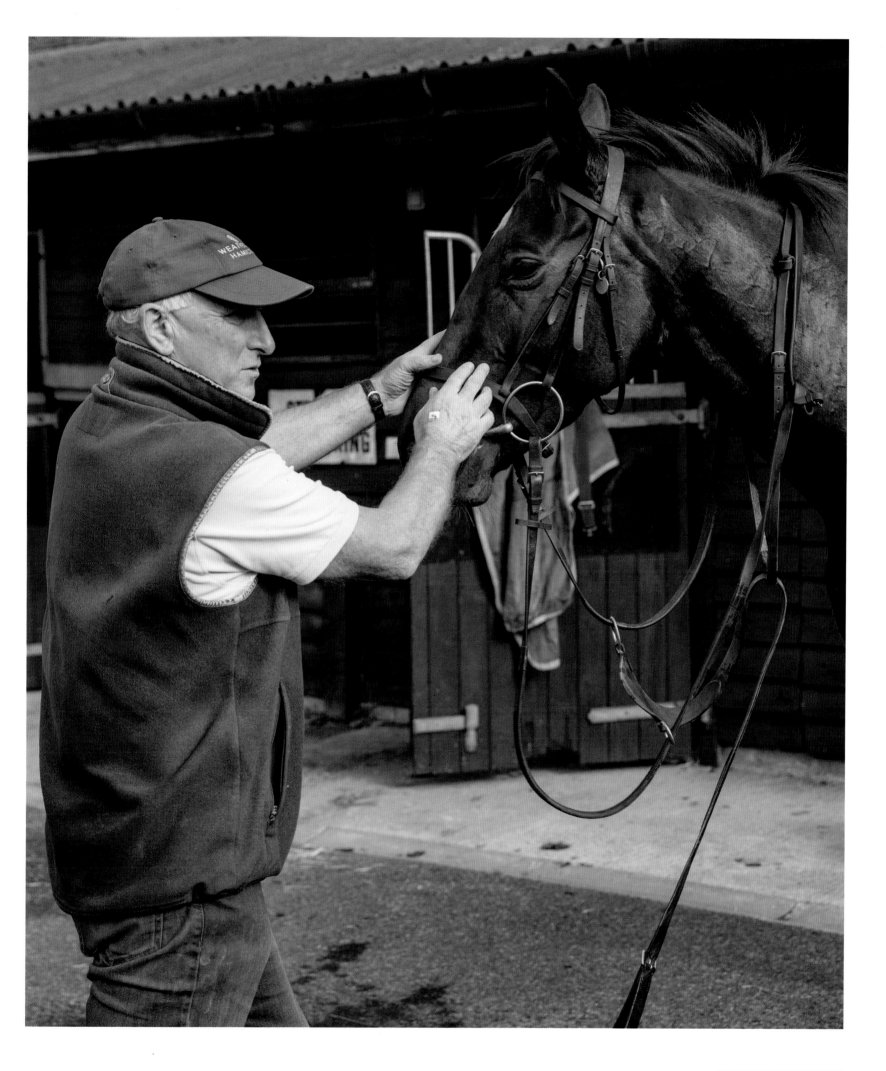

(above) Oliver and Tarnya Sherwood taking a teasing picture break as peaceful stable-yard scenes (top right & right) unfold across the beautifully appointed grounds of Rhonehurst. 'It's important,' Tarnya says, 'to make sure everyone's happy here ... because, at the end of the day, happy staff make happy horses.' (opposite) Jockeys and grooms returning from the morning gallops

Nicky Henderson

Trainer, Seven Barrows, Lambourn, Berkshire

It was old Etonian Nicky Henderson's father Johnny who saved Cheltenham Racecourse from redevelopment in the 1960s. Having ridden from childhood, Nicky worked for Cazenove in his twenties, 'escaping' to become an amateur jockey and assistant trainer to Fred Winter. As of 2017 he has enjoyed fifty-five successes; no trainer has won more races at Cheltenham than Henderson. Among the most notable of his horses have been Remittance Man, winner of the 1992 Queen Mother Champion Chase; and the recently retired Sprinter Sacre, who was unbeaten in ten consecutive outings over fences.

Henderson does not think of himself as unique in the racing world. 'We do a job because we like doing it,' he says modestly, crediting his team of 60 along with his 150 horses. 'I've got a lot of the big owners and a lot of the guys that tend to have nice horses,' he adds. 'I trained for the Queen Mother for all her years ... When she died, the horses were left to the Queen, so she inherited me. She probably didn't want me really! I've known her for years.' Luck has been a factor in his success, 'but things have to go right too. Our job is to make sure that you've got everything in place, so that when [a horse] goes into battle, it has the best chance of winning. We're running it in the right race, in the right conditions, over the right distance. Say you've got all the cards stacked in your favour. Then at least you're starting with a chance.' The amounts of money involved are staggering, but interestingly once horses are thought to have peaked, their value falls, the thinking being that they will not win the major races more than once.

Henderson observes that in his lifetime racing has 'changed dramatically. The funny thing is, [horses are] probably not going any faster. They're not breaking track records every day ... A huge amount of science has come into the whole thing ... We're still building or buying all the new technology we can get. You have to'. As an example he points to a round gallop made of sand from Wexford in Ireland on his property: 'It's very deep ... You can't gallop in that sand; it's for a different type of work. Long, slow work.' He painstakingly judges the conditions of his other gallops, calibrating grass cuts, rainfall and so on every morning and afternoon, every day of the year, rain or shine. Indeed, everything at Seven Barrows is finely tuned and luxurious, 'like staying at The Dorchester. [The horses] get the best of everything. I've always said, if somebody told me that if you fed them gold dust they'd go faster, well then we'd feed them gold dust ... You've got to go with the times. The feed has changed dramatically because now you've got all the nutritionists and scientists. The feed we use is made for us, but it's not far different than the feed anybody else could use; it's not secret recipes'. Comparing his setup to those of others, he adds, 'A lot of the trainers where I started are on a communal gallop that is owned by somebody else. They pay so much a month to use those gallops, but they don't have to do anything about them. There's no maintenance. All they need is a yard; they don't need ... this ridiculous amount of ground.'

Henderson is mindful of the long tradition at Seven Barrows, one of the best private gallops in the business. 'We've got to look after the heritage of this place too, because it's a famous old pad. People like it that way, and it's got history. Let alone the Barrows history; obviously we've got to look after the Barrows [a Bronze Age cemetery]!' It is not all hard work, though. 'We have fun; it's got to be fun,' Henderson says. 'We are in the entertainment business. The owner sends his horse here because he wants to have fun on the racecourse. But he wants to have fun here too ... They'll come down in the morning to see their horses, then we'll go and have lunch, a few drinks, and we'll have a good day.'

(left) The seventeenth-century stable yards at Nicky Henderson's large, elaborate Seven Barrows stud. (opposite) Henderson exudes an air of accomplishment after a hard day's work

Beautiful vistas (above)
celebrate the 400-acre racing
stable's terrain. (right) Take
To Heart, ridden by Dayna
Lee, speeds along one of
the yard's private gallops

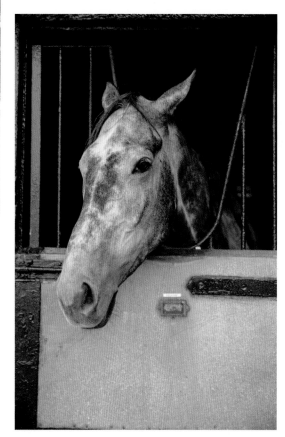

(above) Henderson
hamming it up with a
favourite horse, Altior, and
(right) another prized piece
of equine flesh at Seven
Barrows, Fixe Le Kap

(left & below) Afternoon gallops at Seven Barrows training stables. Horses go out at 8.00 a.m. and 3.00 p.m., every day of every week, every month, every year. Henderson is the only Lambourn trainer who owns his own gallops

Mehmet Kurt

Owner & breeder, Kingwood Stud, Lambourn, Berkshire

'If I have a goal, I always follow it and finish to completion.' So says Turkish-born Mehmet Kurt, who grew up with horses in the city of Ceyhan. His earliest memories are of 'walking between the legs of horses as a toddler. I have ridden for pleasure ever since. I grew up with horses. I was inspired by a mare struggling to keep alive her new-born twin foals. I believe a horse can tell if you are a good person or not; a horse can gauge your intentions. That is why certain people can communicate with horses, and why some jockeys are better than others. Horses have intuition. My method of training respects this'.

Before moving to the UK, Kurt enjoyed success as an owner and breeder in his native country, where he developed the prototype for the Kurtsystem. He describes this system as a revolution in training which prepares horses for racing by developing their muscles and tendons on a conventional all-weather track but safely harnessed onto a specially designed monorail 'car'. Each 'car' provides a readout of the horse's vital signs. The high-tech system is intended to ensure that horses are brought on injury-free.

Due to his father's untimely death, Kurt assumed the leadership of the family's cotton business in 1968 at the age of just twenty-one. A move to Istanbul led him to diversify into media, construction, energy, chemicals, defence, medical, media and property. Kurt continued to invest in his hometown, however, building three schools, converting one of his houses into a public library and transforming the local football team into a professional unit of the Turkish national league. He began work on the Kurtsystem after buying a horse that had been trained in England. 'The other horse in the system, we couldn't train it properly,' he recalls. 'But this horse we bought from England worked well in the system. Only that horse worked. We never gave up.'

In 2011, Kurt left Turkey to set up the technology in England, having experienced 'big problems' at home, which he summarises as 'the politics, the cartel, the oligarchy, everything fighting'. 'I just wanted peace,' he explains. Comfortable on his large estate and a fan of the finer things in life, Kurt has landed squarely on his feet.

Turkish-born Mehmet Kurt (left) in the fold of his complicated automated equine exercise machinery, which he engineered from scratch at a cost of £20 million. (opposite) Far from the madding crowd and shorn of technology, an inquisitive neighbour seeks attention from pesky photographers

Beaufort Hunt

Badminton House, Badminton, Gloucestershire

Located on the Badminton Estate in South Gloucestershire, the Beaufort Hunt is one of four great ancestral packs in England. Hounds have been in the uninterrupted possession of the Dukes of Beaufort, descending from father to son, since 1640, with pedigree records dating from the mid-eighteenth century; the furthest back an individual hound can be traced is fifty-four generations to 1743. This makes the foxhound one of the most chronicled animals in the world today and explains why the bloodline is in demand across the world. The hounds' consistent size and quality owe much to the selective breeding programme carried out by the 10th Duke for sixty years. The hunt's roots also date back to 1640, when the Marquis of Worcester hunted mainly deer.

The Beaufort is one of the few remaining private packs although it has basically been financed by subscription since the mid-twentieth century; post-World War II it became too popular, and too expensive, for the Duke to fund it himself. The Beaufort is no stranger to controversy. In 1999, hunt monitors from the International Fund for Animal Welfare discovered manmade fox earths on land used by the hunt. One year later, the Committee of Inquiry into Hunting with Dogs in England and Wales, chaired by Lord Burns, concluded that hunting with dogs 'seriously compromises the welfare' of foxes, deer, hares and mink. It also noted that between six and eight thousand jobs would

be lost if hunting was banned – half the number suggested by some pro-hunt groups. IFAW's hunt monitors went on to film the Beaufort's official terrier man leaving pheasants and chickens outside manmade fox earths. A short time later, the hunting bill left the committee stage with the so-called 'utility' and 'cruelty' tests toughened up; MPs amended the bill to include hare hunting under the ban. In 2004 the ban passed into law and received royal assent.

Since then, hunts have been obliged to use artificial scent. In light of the ban, the Beaufort set out new rules so that they could carry on, including statements that 'we intend to carry out only legal activities', that 'Farmers, Subscribers, Members and Followers have been informed to this effect', and that, 'Along with other hunts, we regard this as a temporary ban. We will continue to campaign to prove that this ban is detrimental to animal welfare.' The Beaufort continues to organise point-to-points, charity races and hunts, and a pony club. 'Frankly speaking,' notes Captain Ian Farquhar, one of the Beaufort's Masters, 'one of the stupidest things about the 2005 Act is that when they made fox hunting illegal, it had absolutely nothing to do with animal welfare whatsoever.' The scent of politics, many fox hunters contend, can be traced to contemporary urban-rural divides. 'Class,' says Farquhar, 'has everything to do with the controversy surrounding hunting with the horse.'

(left) Riders and hounds await the order to begin the chase, as Captain Ian Farquhar, Joint Master of the Beaufort Hunt, contemplates the moment with Neil Starsmore, second whipper-in, who is responsible for controlling the hounds. In accord with the Beaufort livery, the huntsman and whippers-in all wear green, while other huntsmen and women (subscribers) wear a Beaufort blue coat with buff facings

(opposite) Iona Stokes (ten) on her pony Pippa, waiting for the huntsman's call alongside her father. Ben Elery (left), a trainer whipper-in, cracks the whip as riders and hounds (below) move off

(opposite) Keeper of the Hounds Nick Hopkins stands guard as Trish Richards (right) awaits his command. 'I'm the oldest person on the hunt,' Richards jokes, riding with a group of a hundred others

Captain Ian Farquhar

Joint Master of the Beaufort Hunt, Badminton, Gloucestershire

When asked to describe the enjoyment of riding a horse, Captain Ian Farquhar replies, 'That is a question that people have been asking each other for thousands of years.' He describes his own introduction to the sport this way: 'We were expected to ride because our fathers expected that we would do, because it was a vehicle with which you could play polo, you could hunt, you could race-ride. Then eventing became quite popular, but that was rather a new game ... In my day, the games were race-riding, polo and mainly hunting. Hunting was a sort of religion.' Farquhar dismisses the 2005 hunting ban as 'pure politics – it was Labour, socialist-party politics ... against what they thought [of as] aristocratic countrymen ... which is absolute bollocks, because it's right the way through the countryside, from the farm worker up, and so it has nothing to do with that whatsoever. But that was the Labour perception, that it was a rich man's game'. Like many pro-hunt activists, he believes that the ban has been 'completely detrimental to the wellbeing of the fox'.

Hunting with a horse, says Farquhar, involves both taking exercise and putting your life at risk, 'which is the adrenalin'. When the ban came in, he notes, 'there were two things that we were desperate to keep going. One is our love of our foxhounds. I could talk a great deal about our love of the foxhound. It's the most extraordinary animal, probably the most carefully bred animal in the world ... going back to Norman, Egyptian times, goodness knows what ...The Egyptians had the gazehound, which was the greyhound and the lurcher; they hunt by sight. The Normans brought over the Talbot, which was the first hound that hunted by nose, which is when hunting by nose started ... It was staghounds until about the mid-1700s, when they changed to fox. And they changed to fox because the fox was more difficult to hunt and gave them a better, more exciting run. It tested the huntsman to a greater degree than the stag did ... because you can't see it [and] it doesn't smell as much. A deer smells much stronger than a fox.'

Farquhar describes his relationship with his dogs as his 'complete passion'. His father, grandfather and great-grandfather bred English foxhounds, and he has continued the tradition since leaving the army. Despite the ban, he says, 'they still love to hunt. The inherent trait of the English foxhound (and the Welsh) is you're trying to breed in this conformation that means that it is capable of running up to 100 miles a day, quite fast ... And so physically, it's got to have that conformation. Its feet have got to be right, its body has got to be right, its back has got to be powerful, it's got to have the conformation of an athlete ... A foxhound is an athlete, the same as a Derby winner is an athlete ... The characteristics that you also require as well as the physical ability is the temperament, and this is the fascination of the foxhound: their biddability. It actually likes the person that it's working for, it's handle-able, it's got the biddability, and it wishes to stay as a pack, but it's also got the individual trait that when it's hunting it does its own thing.'

Farquhar notes the inherent democracy of hunting, saying, 'It includes all levels of society, from age eight to eighty-eight ... that was another Labour Party misunderstanding ... You take a village – we're sitting outside Sopworth, which actually is now lost to dairy farms, which is a great pity, because that's the way the country is going, because dairy isn't making money. When it was just a small village, and everybody in that village, whether they work in London, whether they come down, or whether they're a rich man or just a complete cottager and they're working for the council, they're all mates. They're all friends.'

(opposite) Captain Ian Farquhar and close friend and hunt follower Fi Mitchell ham it up with their dogs. (right) The ancient oak has given shelter to many a rider over its centuries of life; Farquhar takes a break beneath it with his lurchers Bosworth and Bracken. 'I spent my life breeding the English foxhound,' he muses. 'The hounds that you saw today can trace their ancestry and pedigree back for fifty-nine generations'

Nick Gauntlett

Event rider, Chescombe Farm Stud, Chipping Sodbury,
South Gloucestershire

International event rider Nick Gauntlett owns a livery and trains horses not far from Badminton. 'Living here I was very lucky,' he says of his childhood. 'Neither of my parents rode at all ... My sister asked if we could go for riding lessons, so for a long time we rode at the local riding school. I only started when I was eleven, so quite a late starter compared to most. We eventually got a pony on loan, then one of our own. In 1992, I was asked to be a slip collector on the cross-country course at Badminton Horse Trials ... It's like being a ball boy at Wimbledon, I suppose. You ride your pony to all the jumps, where the officials on the jumps mark on a bit of paper where all the competitors jumped clear, or not, or what they did. You have to collect the score sheets and take them back to the office.' Gauntlett was fourteen at the time. 'My memory tells me that I was sat on my pony looking up at the jumps, wondering how anybody could ever jump them,' he laughs. 'At the end of the day, we went for a paddle in the Badminton lake, and that was as close as I came for a very long time to jumping a fence. It ignited something in me, I guess: to want to understand something about the sport ... Twelve or fifteen years later, I had my first ride round there myself.' He notes how iconic some of the Badminton jumps have become: 'We have for example the Vicarage Vee, or Huntsmans Close, or The Lake. Being sponsored by Mitsubishi ... every year, you jump the back of a Mitsubishi pick-up. That's quite cool ... To ride round here and to jump these fences ... is quite special.' Badminton was formed in 1949, but every year different course designers 'put their own mark on it, so the course changes'.

Gauntlett believes that nerves are 'a very healthy thing, and controlling them is part of any top sportsman's makeup. In the few hours before you ride the horse, you wonder what on earth you are doing, but as you get to the start – probably you've walked the course four times – you're prepared. You have a bit of a plan in your mind. Unless you're very early to go, you've probably watched a few people go so you've got a good idea of what is happening'. At a course like Badminton, 'you'd think that the depth and intensity of the crowd is going to distract [the horses], but they very rarely get distracted. What we as riders have to do for the horses is to try and keep them confident. Some of these jumps – they are half a ton of animal, they could easily go round these fences or just stop; they don't have to do what we want them to do. They do it because they believe in us and trust us, and they've got a big heart and they want to please us. In return, our job as riders is to not let them down'. By the time horses get to Badminton, 'they've had five years' worth of training at least, so they're fairly tuned in. I teach a lot of body language and things like that, and I would say a lot more travels down the rein to the horse's mouth than you'd ever believe'. Asked whether horses enjoy jumping, Gauntlett replies, 'If they didn't, they wouldn't keep doing it. Great horses definitely know that they're great horses; they enjoy the limelight. You only have to see them when the cameras start clicking and they prick their ears as if to say, "Yes, I was good there!"'

(opposite) Nick Gauntlett leads his horse Cairnside Sir Alex through the stable yard before his daily practice jumps (right) at his family-run farm and stables near Chipping Sodbury, South Gloucestershire. 'My memory,' he laughs, 'tells me that I was sat on my pony looking up at the jumps, wondering how anybody could ever jump them!'

Kim Bailey

Trainer, Thorndale Farm, Withington, Gloucestershire

'I spent two years in Australia when I was a kid,' remembers Kim Bailey. 'I worked with a guy there. We used to talk about what we wanted to do ... My goal was to win the Grand National, his was to own a chain of restaurants. When I won the Grand National, I got a letter saying, "Kim Bailey, The trainer of the Grand National winner, England". Took ten days to arrive. Inside it said, "I've only known one Kim Bailey. Your dream's come true!"' A trainer in jump racing since 1979, Bailey has in fact achieved all of the 'big three': the Grand National, the Cheltenham Gold Cup and the Champion Hurdle. Bailey prides himself on creating a safe, relaxed and professional environment using traditional methods and with a small, close-knit team. His 1,000-acre farm is home to sixty-three stables, all-weather gallops, a round sand gallop, a loose school and staff accommodation. He also writes a daily blog. As a distraction from 'dealing with people all the time', he enjoys fishing.

'Every year is a new season,' Bailey muses. 'Every year, you start from scratch again, and as a result you're back to the bottom of the pile ... It is very levelling, but life is very levelling ... You can't live on memories; you've got to keep going for the future ... My job's like running a school. You're dividing yourself into a fine balancing act to keep everybody happy.' It costs £23,000 a year to have a horse in training, of which Bailey's share is normally half. The ups and downs can take their toll: 'Every time ... I have a horse running for an individual, I get nervous, because it's my job and my reputation on the line. So when you're having a bad time, when the horses are sick and they're not running to their best ability, it's a pretty depressing sport to be involved in ... The highs are huge because when you win the big races ... you're a hero for that day... Then the following day something goes wrong and you're a villain again.'

Bailey currently has seventy-five horses in training, some of which he bought in order to sell them on. He admires their different personalities, joking that 'you have a bond for a certain horse that perhaps annoys you, or does something which irritates you, or does something which pleases you every time you see it'. The diminution of England's equine population is a source of real sadness, but he remains captivated by racing. 'For some extraordinary reason,' he notes, 'Cheltenham [not far from Withington] has been the pinnacle of our racing sport for a very, very long time, ever since National Hunt racing has been involved, for two hundred years or whatever ... We have a slight problem, because everything's geared to four days ... One of the trainers in Newmarket told me, "Kim, I can go and buy a horse for £200,000, £300,000, as a yearling. I cannot guarantee it will win ... at Catterick. But a guy can spend the same amount of money on a horse that's won races in France, Germany, England or Ireland, and the chances are if it's healthy, it will get to Cheltenham." So therefore they can put themselves into their tweed suit, take their box, take their friends, knowing that all things being healthy, their horse will be there. Which they can't guarantee in any other sport.' What's in it for Bailey? 'I get 10 per cent if the horse wins, I get the kudos of being involved in a big race ... and a lot of people come in to see me as a result! And ... there's the roar of the crowd!'

(left) Thorndale Farm stables during early-morning prep. (opposite) Kim Bailey watches eagle-eyed as his horses canter past on their morning gallops against a backdrop of moody West Country skies in the thrall of late autumn

(left) Horses and riders lost in deadly concentration and speed climb towards the top of the gallops. (opposite) Riders chat as friends and competitors, having tested their mettle against the strength of their competitors' mounts and the horsemanship of their close-knit fraternity of riders and grooms. 'Friendship is friendship,' quips one, 'but when it comes to winning, nothing gets in the way'

A horses (right) getting hosed down after returning to the stables before being put back into its box until next time

(following spread) Everything comes down to the horses' courage, stamina, character and training when facing hurdles of multi-coloured jump poles

The King's Troop Royal Horse Artillery

Woolwich, Greenwich, London

The King's Troop Royal Horse Artillery form HM The Queen's ceremonial saluting battery and have been based at stables in Woolwich since 2012. Their purpose-built training facility, designed by Morgan Sindall, Buro Happold, RPS Group (Landscape) and KWA equine consultants, houses 140 horses. Facilities include outdoor training areas, an indoor riding school, a veterinary clinic, a saddlers' workshop, a tailors' workshop and the largest blacksmith's forge in the British Army. Biomass boilers burn the 40 ton of waste produced by the stables each week.

Following their move to Woolwich, the troop's World War I field guns were returned to the Royal Arsenal, where they had been built, and the Royal Artillery, for whom they were made. The Troop's soldiers drive a team of six horses that pull each of the six guns. They also mount HM The Queen's lifeguard at Horse Guards each summer. After World War II and the mechanisation of the last batteries of horse-drawn artillery, King George VI decreed that a

troop of horse artillery should be preserved to participate in ceremonies of state. Accordingly the Troop was re-formed in 1946 at Shoeburyness in Essex. HM The Queen declared that the name 'The King's Troop' would be retained in honour of her father.

The Troop's duties include the firing of royal salutes in Hyde Park and Green Park on royal anniversaries and state occasions; providing a gun carriage and team of black horses for state and military funerals; and performing the famous musical drive around the country. All members, whether male or female, are trained as fighting soldiers, and throughout the Afghanistan campaign augmented other units deploying overseas. Prior to a salute or parade, it takes fifteen cans of wood polish, seven tubes of metal polish, a can of linseed oil, four cans of penetrating oil and thirteen hours to turn out a gun and limber. Due to the guns' age, the majority of parts can no longer be sourced and must be hand-machined by soldiers from the Royal Electrical Mechanical Engineers.

(opposite) The King's Troop Royal Horse Artillery's 13-pounder guns, passed down from World War I, are now only used on ceremonial duty. (above) Two commanding officers lead the Troop in a magnificent display of synchronised horsemanship

Monty Roberts

Horse whisperer, Guildford, Surrey

'If you ask me, "Do you feel like most eighty-two-year-olds you meet?" I'd say no. Most eighty-two-year-olds I meet, they've given up ten years before.' So says Monty Roberts, an eternally busy man of Cherokee/Persian/Irish/Indian descent who was born in California and now works across the globe, spending much of his time in the UK. 'I still feel like I can do almost anything until I start doing it and then it doesn't feel like I can,' he jokes.

Known around the world for his ground-breaking training techniques eschewing any hint of violence, Roberts takes pleasure in the fact that his method has been adopted internationally, with, for example, polo improving 20 to 30 per cent in the last five years thanks to greater speed, increased goals and fewer accidents. 'Western [riding] is taking on my concepts,' he notes. 'We're still waiting for the show jumpers, and we're waiting for the dressage people, but that's happening too.' In competitions he notes a subtle but clear shift towards recognising the overarching importance of harmony between horse and rider.

'I relish all of my friends and the people that support me, but there's a lot of very, very violent enemies out there that don't want me around at all,' the horse whisperer says. A survivor of childhood domestic violence, he works with ex-veterans, trauma victims, youth at risk and prisoners with the horse as principal therapy. 'The horse is all body language, but about 70 per cent of what we say is body language anyway, so [body language in horses and humans is] the same,' he observes. 'From four years of age I knew violence. And the violence that I knew, I knew from the very man that was supposed to protect me in life: my father. My poor mother was so frightened, she hid me. Ginger's

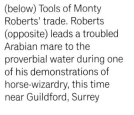

(below) Tools of Monty Roberts' trade. Roberts (opposite) leads a troubled Arabian mare to the proverbial water during one of his demonstrations of horse-wizardry, this time near Guildford, Surrey

manger had a lot of hay and she would put me under the hay so he couldn't find me.' Roberts had started riding Ginger at the age of two.

'In Salinas, California, where I was raised with my father, we had a thousand box stalls. They were drafted by the government to intern Japanese families in 1941 ... I'm already doing stunts in movies, I'm already showing every weekend in competitions ... I never went to grammar school. I went only to take the tests because legally you had to take the tests, show your learning like the other kids.' Roberts had been taught to shoot by an uncle so that he could provide venison for the family and for campers and other visitors. He came up with a plan to shoot his father – but realised that continuing the cycle of violence was not the path he wanted to follow. Instead he went to university, first in California, specialising in behavioural sciences, and then in Zurich. There he learned that, unlike most people, his heart rate slowed when he spoke in front of an audience rather speeding up. 'Audiences is where I wanted to be!' he laughs. This realisation also informed his calming approach to working with horses – and to fostering nearly fifty children at his home in California.

In 1989 Roberts found himself being observed while working at Windsor by HM The Queen. 'I'm there five days, twenty-three horses, each one took its first saddle and first rider in less than thirty minutes,' he recalls. 'I was only supposed to have her for one hour on Monday morning, but she said, "I can't leave here." The first afternoon, I get back and there's a truck outside with these two wild horses in there, and they put them in and Sir John Miller [former Equerry to the Queen] goes in to introduce me and one of the stallions runs him out of the pen!' Within thirty minutes Roberts had a rider on the horse. The Queen said, 'I want you to go on the road now for one month; I'm already booking you in twenty-one cities, ninety-eight horses I want you to do.' Her own horses took up the first five days. 'Twenty-one cities ... and no failures.'

Roberts says he 'would like to be remembered for being born in 1935 when for six thousand years, the only way we worked with horses was violence. You can cut it however you want; you can say, "My great-grandfather was before that time, and he was the greatest horseman." [Truth is,] we used violence for every horse broken before 1935. After 1935 there was the birth of a young man who, through violence to him, decided there was a better way. I would like to be known for just starting that vehicle to move in a different direction'.

Kelly Marks

Intelligent Horsemanship, Lambourn, Berkshire

The daughter of jockey Douglas Marks, Kelly Marks was a successful show jumper as a teenager, 'funded on a shoe-string budget and living mainly on toast'. She moved into racing in her twenties, to earn money. In 1995 she retired from racing after winning the Ladies European Championship. Marks first encountered horse whisperer Monty Roberts in a petrol station in 1993. After helping to write his first books, she put together some courses following his methods. Working internationally, she addresses such problems as refusing to load in a horsebox, bucking, spooking and biting.

'Sometimes I think things can be drawn to you,' Marks muses. 'It's a great advantage if the person that you love most in the world, you copy them.' Together with her dad she went to watch Roberts at work. 'That's the world's greatest horseman,' Douglas Marks told his daughter. Kelly started teaching in Oxfordshire, and it was during a student trip to France that she met Roberts by chance. 'There's a Zen saying,' she notes. '"When the student is ready, the teacher will appear."' It was at the suggestion of HM The Queen that Roberts set up courses with Marks to teach his method.

When dealing with horses, Marks explains, 'It's not just what you do, it's how you are ... It's knowing what's correct for a horse and what isn't, but it's really important, your pulse rate and how you are in yourself ... Originally nobody knew what it was, they knew that some people were better ... horsemen, but they couldn't measure it. Now we can see that it's how you move, how you use your eyes ... Monty is totally incompetent with a computer, but the horse doesn't care about that.'

Kelly Marks (left) alongside a stone-cold canine guarding the entrance to her Lambourn home and stables. (right) Marks with her favourite mare, Jack, resting in the lush rolling fields of Berkshire, one of England's most beautiful counties

The Household Cavalry

Knightsbridge, London

The Household Cavalry consists of the Life Guards and the Blues and Royals (nicknamed the Tin Bellies), the British Army's most senior regiments. Its members are seen both on the battlefield and carrying out ceremonial duties at home. Their members' statement specifies that 'the Household Cavalry are the Trusted Guardians who directly serve their Monarch and their Commander. Regardless of rank, the Nation's trust is founded on their actions. They are the custodian of a reputation built by those who served before. They are trained to excel as a mounted soldier, working in small teams, with mutual respect'.

The Life Guards were founded as four troops of horse guards made up of private gentlemen. For the Anglo-Egyptian War (1882), they formed a Composite Household Cavalry Regiment together with the Royal Horse Guards, which trace their origin back to a force raised by Oliver Cromwell before the second invasion of Scotland in 1661. The parliamentary officers were replaced by Royalists to form the Royal Regiment of Horse (later known as the Blues) to rid the country of residual Republican dissent. In 1890, the regiments were again formed as a Composite Household Cavalry Regiment for the Second Boer War. Other duties have included involvement in conflicts in Afghanistan, Iraq, the former Yugoslavia and Northern Ireland, as well as providing security for the 2012 Olympic Games. The Life Guards are HM The Queen's mounted escort; she holds the title of Colonel-in-Chief. Key State ceremonies include the Queen's Birthday Parade, the Garter Ceremony at Windsor Castle, investitures, the State Opening of Parliament and Remembrance Sunday at the Cenotaph.

Every summer, the Life Guards train near Sandringham in Norfolk. The main aim is to undergo vital instruction without the distraction of public duties. Meanwhile minimum numbers stay behind in London at Hyde Park Barracks. In the morning, the Queen's Life Guard leaves the barracks at 10.28 a.m. (weekdays) or 9.28 a.m. (Sundays) and rides to Horse Guards Parade via the Mall. The Changing of the Queen's Life Guard then takes place on Horse Guards Parade. William Kent, best known as a garden designer, rebuilt Horse Guards in 1758. Barracks, stables and a military HQ, his designs replaced King Charles II's original cavalry site. Influenced by Roman architecture, these neo-Antique buildings remain much as they were in the eighteenth century. For most of the day, the entrance to Horse Guards is secured by two mounted sentries.

The Irish Black is the horse of choice for the Household Cavalry, although other breeds are also incorporated. Shire and Clydesdale horses are used as Drum Horses, for example, carrying huge kettle drums during parades. The horses tend to be geldings of at least 16 hands but are often bigger.

(above) An officer of the Household Cavalry's Blues and Royals out training his troop in the morning sunshine at Hyde Park's riding arena, reserved for their use. (opposite) Two officers of the Household Cavalry's Life Guards returning from an official engagement, dressed in polished cuirasses, buckskins and jackboots – the last originally reinforced against sword blows. Their helmets sport brass and silver fittings as well as long plumes of horse hair; their mounts are all black three-quarter-bred Irish draught horses

(left) The Westbury
(or Bratton) White Horse has
adorned this hill overlooking
an Iron Age fortification
for several hundred years;
nobody knows quite when
it first appeared. It was
restored in 1873, and again
in the early twentieth
century, when its edges
were etched in concrete

Mary King MBE
Eventer, Salcombe Regis, Devon

'I used to take my school homework into the field in the evenings and sit with the horses,' recalls Mary King. 'I just loved it.' Known for being highly competitive and strong-willed, King has a career that spans thirty years. She is the only rider to have competed in six Olympics, the only person to have won five British national titles at Gatcombe, and joins Mark Todd and William Fox-Pitt in holding the record for winning four British Open championships.

King worked for Sheila Willcox, a former European champion, after she left school, learning everything from breaking in young horses to stable management. Converting a couple of cowsheds near her home, she looked after other people's horses, gave riding lessons, and bought and sold horses. To supplement her income, she cleaned, cooked, did garden maintenance and delivered meat for the local butcher. She did not get into eventing until she was about thirteen: 'I went on the Pony Club coach trip to Badminton Horse Trials ... and couldn't believe what I saw – all these shiny horses and shiny riders, and they all seemed so brave, galloping over these huge fences ... and they all seemed so rich ... and ... beyond reach. I was struggling to jump

(below) Mary King at her stables, and (opposite) taking a tea break with her dog Barney and her 'trained' chicken Phoebe in her walled garden

a couple of feet and didn't have the money or the background ... I thought, This is what I want to try and do one day.' King realised her dream when she was twenty-five.

Eventing has different phases: 'You've got the dressage, which is the obedience phase where you're judged on various movements, so that's very much training, obedience, the horse being submissive and calm and listening to the rider; and the cross-country phase, where a good event horse really comes into its own – they love to gallop at speed, and they love the challenge of the cross-country fences.' In three-day eventing, King observes, 'men and women compete on equal terms, and the woman is as good as the man, if not better'.

King competes every weekend during the eventing season, getting up at 'ridiculous times, like 3.00 a.m., to get anywhere. My mother got her HGV licence years ago and she still does most of the driving – she's seventy-three now. Often we will get back at 11.00 p.m. and she'll say, "I'm just off to clean the church," because she took over my father's verger duties when he died'. King has ridden quite literally through thick and thin. 'It was a secret at the time, but I was five and a half months pregnant with Emily at the European Championships in October 1995. I kept very fit, so it didn't show, although I did let out my jacket a bit, and I was riding King William, who I knew was the safest cross-country horse in the world. Obviously my mum and David [King's husband] knew, and I had to tell the team doctor because there would be a medical. I came away with a team gold and individual bronze medal.' On the minus side, she describes 'riding a young horse called King George in a field up the road when a pheasant flew out of the hedge. King George bucked, and I fell and landed on the back of my neck. I just couldn't get up. I eventually managed to roll onto my side and, holding my head in my hands, get up. My friend took me to hospital, and they X-rayed me and said I had whiplash, but when I went out riding again my head felt very loose. A week later I went to a consultant who told me I had broken my neck. I had to have an operation to realign the bones in my neck. My surgeon said, "Don't ride for eight weeks and don't fall off for ten weeks!" I thought he was brilliant!'

(left) Mary King with her horse King's Temptress visiting her mother in the churchyard at St Mary's and St Peter's Church in Salcombe Regis. It was there that King first came into contact with horses. Her father was the verger when she was a little girl; she learned to ride on the parish priest's horses. 'I bred King's Temptress to the top level of our sport,' she says. 'She was my reserve horse for the London Olympics.' (above) King out on a late-afternoon stroll on a hill overlooking the Bristol Channel

The Exmoor Pony

Emma & David Wallace, Breeders, Anchor Exmoor Ponies,
Exmoor National Park, Somerset

Anchor Exmoor Ponies was started by industrialist Francis William 'Frank' Green, who purchased Old Ashway Farm and its moorland allotments in the late 1920s along with half of the Exmoor ponies that grazed there. The remaining half of the herd was owned by Sir Thomas Acland, whose family had bred ponies in the Royal Forest since 1767. All of the ponies were identified by an anchor-shaped brand, thought to denote royal property. Eventually Green purchased the remaining half of the herd and, when they were threatened with being slaughtered for horsemeat during World War II, brought them off the moor to safety. Their breeding and management has continued through several generations of his family, and is now under the oversight of David and Emma Wallace. The Anchor herd are currently shown in hand, with several coming out under saddle to contend at county shows, even (with new owners) qualifying for the Horse of the Year Show and Olympia.

'They don't usually have to do extreme heat in this country, but they do the cold,' Emma notes of the breed. 'They have a double coat. They have whorls on their faces [and] fatty pads above their eyes to shed water. They have what's called a "snow chute" of a tail, which sits well into their backside so that the water is shed off them as quickly as possible. They can stand in twenty-four hours of rain and still have a dry tummy because the water has just run off the sides.' Their unusual bite makes it possible for Exmoor ponies to nip at branches and gorse. First recorded in the Domesday Book, they are, like New Forest ponies, semi-feral. The Exmoor, whose breed society was formed in 1921, has been given 'endangered' status by the Rare Breeds Survival Trust, and 'threatened' status by the Livestock Conservancy. They are usually dark bay in colour, with pangaré (mealy) markings around muzzle and underbelly, and stand 11.1 to 12.3 hands.

'In essence we have about 25 per cent of the world's genetics in the herd with our eight founder lines,' Emma explains. 'Until the tractor came along, your typical Exmoor farmer would have ridden an Exmoor pony to gather his sheep and cattle off the moors,' adds David. Even the local postman rode one on his rounds. 'Now their purpose is conservation grazing,' Emma notes. 'They are amazing at keeping the countryside looking as it does … They keep the shrub under control by nipping at the gorse and stripping out the mats of rubbish grasses on the hill.' And, David explains, 'You can go round the coastlines of Britain on foot, and you will come across Exmoor ponies in Northumberland, in Cornwall, in Sussex, because people like the National Trust have discovered what an asset they are.' Farming Exmoor's hilly terrain may make it 'very difficult to make a living', concludes Emma, 'but in the National Park, it's a very important thing to do'.

(opposite) Somerset farmer-
breeders Emma and David
Wallace ('Mom and Pop'
as they like to refer to each
other). (above) Exmoor
ponies sharing secrets

(left) Exmoor ponies range freely across the moors, helping to maintain the ecosystem by munching the coarse, prickly gorse

Susan George
Breeder, Georgian Arabians, Exmoor National Park, Somerset

'I'm a very instinctive person,' says actor Susan George. 'I like to do everything at the drop of a hat.' George, who has been breeding Arabians for more than twenty years, has been a horse lover all her life. The success of Georgian Arabians, she says, is the direct result of her late husband Simon MacCorkindale's 'passion, courage, strength and tenacity'.

George and MacCorkindale were living in Northampton in the 1980s; the move to Exmoor marked a major change on many levels. 'I absolutely loved riding, being with my mother and sharing that time,' she says of her childhood. 'Then I had a long period without horses. And then, at twenty-two years of age, I had a boyfriend in California [singer Jack Jones]' with whom she would ride at the weekend. 'I rode this little mare [Schatzi] that I really adored. She was seven-eighths Arab ... My boyfriend bought her for me as a birthday present. [At the time] I was a nomad, working, in a suitcase all the time. But every time I came back to the field where I kept her ... she would spin round in the way Arabs do, with her big eyes and her mane floating in the air and her tail over her back, and she would just charge up to the fence to see me. That kind of bond, that kind of big-time loyalty, is something I always associate with Arabians. Once you have that loyalty, it never goes away; it never breaks. She had this feeling for me, and I did for her, but I felt that it wasn't good enough for my part. I felt really selfish that I came so infrequently ... People say that horses don't think and know and feel like us ... but I think they are thinkers, especially Arabs ... And they'll come back and get you if you fall off.'

The fact that Arab horses connect with particular people 'for life' is why 'it's so hard as a breeder', George notes. 'I realised this later down the line, when I really hadn't given thought to the fact that when you breed horses, you are going to have to part with horses ... I really didn't think about the fact that when I got bigger and began to breed, I perhaps would not like some of the people that I had to part with the horses for ... When I think about the consideration I have in terms of breeding what I want to achieve in structure and bone and body and type, all the recognition that I now have for the breed and what I want to put back into the breed and see go forward in the future of the breed ... I look first at structure and secondly at bloodlines, paperwork.'

George and MacCorkindale married three years after they first met. Recognising the 'big, passionate' importance of horses to his new wife, MacCorkindale said, 'When we are in one place and we can really dedicate time to this, and you can give the hundred per cent that you wanted to give to Schatzi, we'll do it.' In 1985 the pair become film producers, returned to England and 'made the decision to start the farm. I searched the United Kingdom to find this one mare ... I was looking for an older, bomb-proof riding horse, to replace — not replace, but to be another Schatzi for me. I ended up at somebody's farm, they were a show-training farm, and they did this incredible thing which I do now, which is these big shows called in-hand shows. Trainers run with horses; it's magnificent to watch. If people come to our shows expecting to see something like any other horse show in the world, they leave open-mouthed. It's show business in a way. There's music and lots of noise, and the horses respond to the noise. Arabians love noise ... With the sound comes the snorting and blowing ... They make this incredible noise ... expressing, "Look at me! I am beautiful!" So I came to this farm and I saw this in this big barn ... and the horses performed in this exuberant, charismatic fashion, and I'm looking for a steady riding horse that I can go up the lanes with ... I felt the excitement and I could see how the real beauty and magic of the Arabian horse was shown in this free-spirited fashion'.

George 'used to be a party animal' herself but enjoys her own company more now. 'I go out to something perhaps two or three times a year and really enjoy it,' she says. 'But I love my space and I love my horses. Nothing could be better for me than what I have.' She derives solace from her horses, who 'give back, far more than one could ever give them, all the time'.

(opposite) Several of Susan George's Arabian horses grazing in her stud farm's paddocks, while (right) their owner luxuriates in the contrast of manmade colours and natural hues

(left) Susan George with her
grooms, allowing one of her
horses to take a bite of her
hat. Other fine examples
of her Arabian stud at rest
(above), and cavorting
in their large paddocks
(opposite)

The River Barle (right) outside Barleton in Somerset. (below) A lane emblematic of the English countryside, where thousands of miles of byways, some as narrow as a horse-drawn carriage, wind across the land affording enchanting perspectives

Tim & Jonelle Price

Event riders, Mere Farm, Marlborough, Wiltshire

Born in New Zealand, Tim and Jonelle Price relocated to the UK in 2005, setting up camp at Mere Farm in Wiltshire – 'a little slice of New Zealand in the heart of England'. Jonelle had ditched a law degree at Canterbury University in favour of eventing; Tim had always ridden, having grown up on a horse farm. By 2000 he had focused on show jumping and competed in his first World Cup. Twelve years later, Jonelle won team bronze with Flintstar (a horse bred by Tim's parents) at the London Olympics. After Tim's 2014 win at Luhmühlen, he and Jonelle became the first husband and wife on a New Zealand World Equestrian Games team. As of 2017, Tim was second place in world eventing rankings.

At the lower levels of eventing, 'the women far outweigh the men, but once you get up to élite level, I would say it's dominated by men,' notes Jonelle. 'The attributes that are required to be one of the best in the world are quite tough – it's not for the faint-hearted – so maybe that favours men ... With women, often their career is altered by having children ... and their priorities change a little bit.' She and Tim met as teenagers on the eventing circuit. Jonelle was living at

the top of South Island and had to travel long distances for competitions. 'Christchurch, where Tim's from, would have been the hub of horses in the South Island,' she explains, 'so where I was from was quite out of touch.' Tim adds, 'We got to know each other and I chased her for a bit there, and the rest is history ... We definitely reinforce each other. It's been a work in progress over the years. And it's a funny thing, because there have definitely been different chapters to our journey together as horse people. New Zealand was a whole lot of fun, travelling around together and living out of the horse truck for three weeks. Life was very easy ... When we decided to make the big move over here, we did that together, did some fundraising ... We always knew that there was a bigger world out there.' The business model the couple adopted involved 'buying, training horses, training other people, selling horses. Basically any good horse that came along was going to be sold to another top rider, and while that's good because it's money in the bank, it also means that you lose that ride, so you're not actually going to realise the glory on that horse, if you like'. 'It wasn't ultimately how we wanted the business to be,' Jonelle interjects, 'but we had to start somewhere.'

The couple found Mere Farm by a stroke of luck. 'The farm when we took it on, you wouldn't recognise it. It was completely run-down, it was a dive,' remembers Jonelle. 'It had been a good, well-run place at some point in the past, and then had done nothing for a number of years except be run into the ground. When we got there, there wasn't a single fence standing, there was no electricity in the yard, or anywhere. It was dark and dingy and horrible,' adds Tim. The owners had just bought the place but did not want any involvement with running the place, so the Prices worked off their rent doing it up. 'We had five horses; we owned 100 per cent of every one of those horses,' Tim recalls. 'Now we own thirty horses and we own 100 per cent of two horses. The other horses have syndicates, owners of all sorts of dilutions.'

'It's a great leveller, this sport, because you can win one day and be on the dirt the next,' Tim notes. 'It's the same with the owners. They can have a very special horse that can win, but next time out, disaster can strike. But you ride that wave, you ride that dip, and you come out next time and hopefully go well again.'

Tim and Jonelle Price (left) taking a break with their Labrador in the grounds of their stables near Marlborough. (opposite) Tim Price and his Irish sport horse Boleybawn Fernhill testing their dressage skills against mirrored competition. 'It's a great leveller, this sport, because you can win one day and be in the dirt the next,' Price observes

(opposite) Jonelle Price inspecting her horses in the main yard of her large stables, which date from the seventeenth century. The Prices live with their baby son Otis, their horses, chickens and the odd spotted pig or two roaming at large. 'We're a big happy family,' Jonelle says. (right) Tim Price taking a late-afternoon canter amid the stud farm's arboreal splendour

(left) A picture speaks a thousand words as one of the Prices' inquisitive horses, a Dutch-bred gelding named Kalypso Du Buisson Z, welcomes a tiny intruder: a new chick on parade

Lucy & Ben Sangster

Breeders, Manton, Marlborough, Wiltshire

'I'm an absolute stickler; I lead by example. If you want to have good staff, you can't have them thinking that you're all asleep in bed while they're working. It doesn't work like that.' So says breeder (and former model) Lucy Sangster, whose estate includes a racehorse training centre, gallops, horseboxes, a manor house and its own hamlet. Her father-in-law Robert Sangster bought the estate, built in the 1860s, in 1984. Since the Sangsters have had Manton (greatly reduced in size since Robert's death), they have had over fifty Group 1 winners. Robert Sangster changed the face of thoroughbred racing in the 1970s, winning the Derby and the Prix de l'Arc de Triomphe twice and helping to create a global bloodstock brand with the Coolmore Stud in Ireland. The stables at Manton have turned out fifty Classics winners over their 150-year history.

Lucy suspects that she would not have become involved with horses had she not met Ben. 'Ben worked for his father,' she explains. 'He was involved with the horses on a day-to-day basis, and then when we got married in 1990 we moved down here and have been here ever since.' She finds thoroughbred breeding and racing 'addictive', and is, not surprisingly, always on the lookout for a winner.

'There are two big horses at the moment,' she notes. 'One is Frankel and the other is Nathaniel. They have both had their first three-year-old crops this year. Both of them have been very, very good horses, and they're looking like being extremely good stallions. But they could also have a bad year next year ... That's why it's rather like a commodity ... You're hedging your bets on who you breed your foal to, your mare to, and then it has a foal. And the stallion market goes in and out – fashionable, not fashionable. The stallion might have a quiet year then a hot year, prices fluctuate ... If a sire has no two-year-old runners, it's immediately a black point against him.' She mentions Galileo, 'the sire of all sires at the moment', who is owned by Coolmore. A single covering by Galileo costs around £450,000 (there is no artificial insemination in thoroughbred breeding). 'Aidan O'Brien, who's a top Irish trainer, conquered the world this year. He had twenty-six, twenty-seven Group 1 winners, so he beat the all-time record. Of those winners, nineteen were Galileo's and six of the other ones' grandfathers were either by Sadler's Wells [Galileo's sire] or Galileo. So indirectly, bar three horses, every single one of those winners had something to do with either Sadler's Wells or Galileo.'

Breeding, Lucy points out, is 'a game of chance, a big poker game'. The stakes are phenomenal. 'I always say the racing industry is a little bubble of a world because it defies the stock market, money markets, countries that are in trouble. Every year, everyone goes to the sales, wondering what the market's going to be like. Are we going to make our money back, are we going to do this, are we going to do that? And every year it just defies everything.' What can make the difference between large breeders and smaller ones like Manton? 'Because we're small, we probably spend a bit more time with [our horses] than other big studs that don't necessarily have the time,' Lucy notes. 'A lot of horses wouldn't let you go and stand in the paddock with them; they'd be too wild. But because we've always spent a bit more time with them, they're very calm. I don't want to lead round some wild thing that's going to buck and kick me. The more time you spend with them, the more friendly they are towards you ... [The keys to success are] good feed, good mating, good mares. You try and do the best you can.'

Lucy and her husband Ben Sangster (opposite) take pride in their family's successful racing history. Ben's father Robert had over fifty major winners during the 1970s, both nationally and internationally

Manton stud, whose stables (above) date back to the mid-nineteenth century

(following spread) Manton in the autumn

Tom Scudamore

Flat & steeplechase jockey, Bromsash, Ross-on-Wye, Herefordshire

Tom Scudamore grew up in Gloucestershire, the heart of British jump racing. He is the son of eight-time champion jockey Peter Scudamore, and his grandfather Michael won the Grand National in 1959. Educated at Cheltenham College, Tom obtained two A-levels alongside a full-time training schedule. His first flat win was on Nordic Breeze at Warwick in 1998; he was only sixteen. That same year, he had his first steeplechase win with Young Thruster at Newton Abbot Racecourse. His best season was 2013–14, when he amassed a hundred wins.

'My great-grandfather was a farmer,' Scudamore says. 'There's a big hunting scene in rural areas; then you had the point-to-pointing ... I'm not sure when the first races started, but you have recorded meetings in the 1700s. Then in the 1800s ... it was basically two landed gentry saying, "My horse is faster than your horse!"' Today Scudamore earns around £165 per ride. 'Then I'll get 10 per cent of the win prize money and 5 per cent of the place prize money,' he notes. 'Last season I won over a million pounds ... We're making a very comfortable living out of it and we're grateful for that.' This is not true for everyone in racing, of course. 'Unless you're in the top fifteen, maybe even top ten, you're scraping by,' Scudamore explains. 'People are coming out of the racing industry because they can make more money doing other things.'

Scudamore describes his state of mind at the start of a race as 'clinical ... At that moment, my pure feeling is to work out how I can get this horse from A to B in the quickest possible time ... There's no formula; you plan it out, but you've got to have a touch and feel for it as well ... I have an idea in my head of how I want the race to be run and how I can affect it in the best possible way for my horse ... If I get everything right, I will achieve my maximum, and if I'm on the best horse in the race, nine times out of ten that'll win anyway. But what I'm also thinking is that if I do my bit right, and somebody else makes a mistake – this is what I believe separates the best jockeys from the rest: I'm a shark waiting for someone else to make a mistake ... I'm concentrating on certain positions on the track where I want to be, where I want to be going faster, holding on'. A good jockey is familiar with every racecourse in the country. To this knowledge Scudamore adds his awareness of 'all the horses I'm riding against' – a killer combination, as his repeated success makes clear. 'There will be times when you question yourself in the race ... because you'll look ahead and there's a group of successful jockeys ahead. Maybe you got this one wrong? But it's the same in any other major sport. You have to back yourself and believe in yourself ... You know all your competitors, but you're in your own little bubble, and that concentration mustn't be broken.'

What Scudamore loves most about racing is 'that you have to respect everybody involved in it. Obviously you respect the horse, and you respect the people who look after it. There's always that underlining danger, which makes it attractive too ... People working in the yard, people looking after these horses – I have a responsibility to them to perform on the track. If I don't perform, the horses get taken away; they lose their jobs'.

(left) Tom Scudamore and his daughter Myrtle cleaning up outside the stables on his brother's racing stables near Ross-on-Wye. (opposite) Scudamore taking a breather on his thoroughbred Copper Coin after a hard morning's gallop, the horse still frothing at the mouth from vigorous exercise

(left) Tom Scudamore riding another thoroughbred, State Sovereignty, through beautiful Herefordshire countryside along with Kate Hanson, one of the stable managers. (right) Scudamore and his mother Marilyn, who helps run the enterprise, talking horse sense amid the vestiges of autumn

Uffington White Horse

White Horse Hill, Uffington, Oxfordshire

The Uffington White Horse is a prehistoric hill figure formed from deep trenches filled with crushed white chalk. The hill, which forms part of the escarpment of the Berkshire Downs, overlooks the Vale of White Horse, and the site is owned and managed by the National Trust. A Scheduled Ancient Monument, it is also home to two other figures; all three lie beside the Ridgeway, the ancient track that ran from Dorset to the Wash.

The White Horse is Britain's oldest chalk-cut hill figure, dating to the late Bronze or Iron Age (1740–210 BC), and may have been a territorial marker or fertility symbol. The horse-goddess Epona worshipped by the Celts in Gaul had a counterpart in Britain, Rhiannon; perhaps the Uffington White Horse was created by adherents to her cult. Another theory is that it represents a depiction of a 'solar horse', reflecting a belief that the sun was carried across the sky on a horse or in a chariot. Uffington Castle, which occupies the summit of White Horse Hill, is a rare example of a large Iron Age hillfort. Once every seven years from at least 1677 until the late eighteenth century, a midsummer 'scouring festival' was held during which local people cleaned the chalk outlines of the horses and enjoyed a celebratory feast within the hillfort.

The Royal Wessex Yeomanry Ride
Sopworth, South Gloucestershire

There are currently ten listed hunting packs in Gloucestershire, of which the Yeomanry is one. The original meaning of the term *yeomanry* was a group of men who held and cultivated small landed estates; the early history of hunting is thought to have been associated with estate management rather than sport. King Edward II published accounts of foxhunting as early as 1420; its increased popularity coincided with a wane of interest in falconry in the 1600s. In his youth, Henry VIII is said to have worn out eight horses in one day's hunting. By the seventeenth century, fox hunting had become popular among the aristocracy.

Since the 2005 ban, hunts use a set trial for the hounds. Varying in size, the horses jump multiple fences and hedges very much like cross-country and follow the hounds, which are led in turn by the huntmaster. Hunt subscriptions range from a few hundred to several thousand pounds per horse. Added expenses include coats, tack, grooms, transport, vets and, of course, the horse itself. Despite amalgamations and urbanisation, there are more packs of hounds in England today than in 1900, and not one has folded since the ban came in. The onset of fox-hunting season is late August or early September, after crops have been harvested. The season comes to a close as landowners begin preparing the earth for crop production in the spring.

Foxhunting country is diverse and may include meadows, forests, fields and marshes. Prior to the official opening of the season, 'cubbing season' occurs. For several weeks, first-season hounds are taken to the field in the early morning to amass experience and disperse fox cubs over the countryside. Hounds are not kept in the field for extended periods during cubbing season as the huntsman wants only to ensure they are tracking the proper game. Because cubbing season is less formal in nature, hunt members are often invited to ride 'green' mounts so the horses can become acquainted with the hunting environment.

Asked what hunting signifies to her, Yeomanry member Gayle Sturgess replies, 'Adrenalin!' Comparing hunts in other countries, fellow member John White insists that only the Irish are better than the English. 'The Irish economy depends on it, and also they have perfect climate,' he explains. Comparisons notwithstanding, White says he can 'remember some very good hunts on some very good horses. There's nothing like it when you have a really good horse ... It's very, very exciting'.

(right) Ewen Cameron (holding the winner's cup) is congratulated by fellow riders of the Yeomanry Hunt, and by enthusiastic foxhounds

(opposite) A mix of tradition and family fun unites riders, spectators and horses at the Yeomanry Hunt's Saturday meets in the South Gloucestershire countryside (above left & right) Caroline Llewellyn and Celina Hopkins in a quiet moment before the rush of adrenalin that will push horses and riders to jump dangerous fences at a most unreasonable pace. 'It's not about winning but more about taking part,' Hopkins says of hunting

(right) As pleasing as it is to watch the beauty, agility and courage of horseflesh in action, it is often more amusing to look closely at the faces of riders in their various stages of ascent and descent at hair-raising speeds, against bone-breaking obstacles. (below) All is forgotten and forgiven after the exhilaration of the race, at least for those with their mounts still under them

(following spread) A painterly view of the Yeomanry Hunt in action, the attitudes of the riders suggesting that old expression 'Let the Devil take the hindmost!' Surprisingly, riders will dismount to attend to fallen or injured fellow riders

Olympia Horse Show

Hammersmith, London

The Olympia Horse Show is one of Britain's pre-eminent annual gatherings, attracting a wide audience of enthusiasts, the best riders and the finest horses both nationally and internationally. (left) Michael Whitaker showing magnificent horsemanship on Jb's Hot Stuff, and (opposite) Ben Maher on Diva II evidencing grace, agility and control

Olympia first opened its doors in 1886 as the National Agricultural Hall. The horse show was established in 1907, with most participants being of a military background. The idea is thought to have originated with breeder Reginald Gardiner Heaton, who persuaded some friends to organise an international show similar to those in New York, Paris and Brussels. Lord Lonsdale, President of the National Sporting Club of Britain and nick-named 'The Yellow Earl' after the colour of his livery, was the show's first President; the list of directors included prominent sporting patrons from the aristocracy. 'In those great and far-off days almost everyone was horse-minded so it was hardly surprising that great success became the under-taking,' wrote Geoffrey D. S. Bennett in *Horse & Hound* in 1954.

The show was suspended at Olympia during World War II and resurrected in 1947 at White City. Nearly thirty years later, a horse show returned to Olympia courtesy of Heaton and Raymond Brooks-Ward. The London International Horse Show has since become one of the highlights of the equestrian calendar; HM The Queen has visited many times. Events include show jumping, dressage, demonstrations, driving and showing.

Olympia is the only show in the UK to feature International Federation for Equestrian Sports-level jumping, driving and dressage at one event, and participants are the best of the best. Four hundred horses and ponies are brought over, occupying 276 stables and using 32 ton of bedding. Two farriers and eight vets are available throughout the show, which is attended by over eighty-five thousand people annually. The Puissance, the show's key jump, requires a powerful mount and refined technique. The approach varies depending on the rider. 'You must hold your nerve and not go too soon,' observed jumping legend John Whitaker in *Olympia* magazine. Essentially the horse needs to trust the rider, as he can't see what's behind the wall. Olympia's course builder, Bob Ellis, usually sets the Puissance in increments as rounds progress. 'It's all about giving [the horses] confidence at the start,' he told *Olympia* in 2017.

John Whitaker MBE

Equestrian & Olympian, Heyside Farm, Upper Cumberworth, West Yorkshire

In 2017, John Whitaker fell off a horse and was taken to hospital during the London Global Champions Tour on his sixty-second birthday. Seventeen years earlier, he had returned to riding after suffering a life-threatening brain haemorrhage. Seemingly nothing can stand in Whitaker's way when it comes to riding. One of the world's most admired show jumpers, he has competed in dozens of major international championships and collected twenty-four medals at the Olympics and world and European championships. One of his most famous horses, Milton, was the first show-jumping horse to win more than £1 million in prize money. Whitaker also owns an innovative clothing brand for both riders and their mounts.

'I kind of look at myself as a normal Yorkshire farmer,' says Whitaker. 'I suppose I am an elder statesman of the show-jumping world, but I don't think about my age ... We're lucky in this sport: we can carry on competing at my age and still be reasonably successful ... There are actually quite a few older than me still doing it.' Whitaker started riding at the age of six, began competing around nine or ten, and has been competing internationally since he was a teenager.

'I think I'm still a threat when I'm competing,' he laughs. 'They don't say, "Oh, we've only got that old guy coming off, we've only got that old guy to beat." I think, No, I think I can still beat them.' Falling off is an occasional part of the package 'because if you don't take risks, you don't win. And when you take risks, the chances are it can go wrong ... You tend to just go for it. You can see what you have to beat. If somebody takes all the options, all the chances, like turning really short to big jumps and going fast, and if somebody does that and they get away with all the risky turns and all the galloping and they're in the lead, you think, Well, to beat that, I have to go faster than that, obviously ... And you take more risks ... If you're too careful, you don't win'.

Whitaker notes that, unlike many sports, in show jumping 'men and women compete equally ... They're competing for the same prize money – everything's exactly the same ... It's a fact that women are just as good as men in our sport ... They're not as strong ... but horses perform for them, and some horses even perform better for women than men ... It's like a telepathy thing ... There are some horses that my daughter can ride probably better than me, but there are some horses I can ride better than her. Strength comes into it a little bit sometimes, with some horses. With some horses, it's feeling and sensitivity ... whereas if you get one that's a bit strong to ride or a bit lazy, then it probably suits a man better ... You could spend millions, buy a horse, and you ride it and it probably doesn't work because you haven't got the right feeling for each other ... If I take a new horse on ... I say to the horse, "I want to do it this way," and the horse argues and says, "No, I want to do it this way," so somewhere you meet in the middle.'

Whitaker feels fortunate to have had a 'fantastic career'. 'When I was seventeen years old, sixteen years old, I watched show jumping on television, and I thought, I'd like to do that. I never really thought that I would get to the point where it was going to be a profession ... To make a career out of it, that's enough for me, and if I win something along the way then it's been good.'

(previous spread)
A momentary break in stormy January weather reveals a wondrous scene on the road to Westerdale, near the North Yorkshire county line

(opposite) John Whitaker leading his horse Storm through his icy stable yard for a ride on a frigid January morning. (right) A more relaxed Whitaker at the entrance to his stud farm, having survived his morning duties

(right) Rider and horse working together against the elements. Whitaker, who has been riding the six-year-old Storm for a year, describes their relationship this way: 'He goes my way because we started together ... It's a perfect marriage.' Not many relationships would outlive the testing conditions of a Yorkshire winter

Sophie Wells

Paralympian dressage rider, Harby, Newark, Nottinghamshire

'I was born with a disability – amniotic band syndrome – so before birth I lost some of my fingers,' explains Sophie Wells. 'The same thing happened around my legs, but they managed to save them; I had plastic surgery when I was ten days old. But I was always treated by my parents as exactly the same as my younger brother, who was able-bodied, and we were given the same opportunities.' Para-equestrian Wells went on to win three medals at the 2012 Summer Paralympics in London and gold at the 2016 Summer Paralympics in Rio.

Horses came into Wells' life when, as a child, she sat on a pony at a friend's birthday party; soon she was attending her local riding school. In 2001, she started training with Vicki Thompson Winfield in Lincolnshire. During this time Wells was introduced to Harry Dabbs, who was sponsoring Thompson Winfield at the time; Dobbs developed the 'looped' reins that enabled Wells to keep in consistent contact with her horse while riding. In 2008 Wells was reserve for the Beijing Paralympic Games with Touchdown M, who was discovered to be lame at the last minute. This distressing time ultimately led to her impressive partnership with another horse, Pinocchio.

'Because I wasn't treated as though I had a disability, I didn't think I had one as such,' Wells recalls of her early life. 'If anyone said anything, I said, "But I was born like this, just like you were born how you were" ... People hadn't seen it so they didn't know how to respond. I've taken that on and I've gone into schools and tried to ... open [people] up to the fact that while I may look different and I have different challenges, I still want to do the exactly the same as everyone else.' She confesses that she 'only became comfortable' with her disability after London 2012, when it was talked about much more openly than in the past.

Wells is well aware of the fragile aspects of equestrian sport, noting, 'You're only as good as your horse. If you don't have a good horse, it doesn't matter how good a rider you are.' Trust and rapport are essential, 'because you're not fighting a horse with force. You can't physically force a horse to do what you want them to do. You have to use your brain, you have to use communication skills, and build it up over time ... In the stable, they're like my children; I love them. But when we're in the arena and we get on, then we're work partners.'

Paralympian Sophie Wells (left) gossiping with a favoured mount at her stables, and (opposite) in her training arena with her horse

The Caspian Horse

Penny Walster, Breeder, Bathley, Newark, Nottinghamshire

Penny Walster has been a Director, stud owner and manager of the Caspian Horse Society since 2010. It was in 1974 that the earliest Iranian breeding records were handed over to the society's founders for safekeeping; this was also when the first breeding stock arrived in the UK from Iran. Four years later, the society published the first international Caspian stud book, holding details of both early Iranian and British-born horses. In 2011, the European Commission granted the society the status of holding the 'Stud Book of Origin'. The society, now a DEFRA-approved Passport Issuing Organisation for the breed, prevents inbreeding by keeping detailed records of horses and by advocating the cyclic crossing method, where each mare is bred with a different stallion to its relatives.

The Caspian Horse has a short, fine head with wide forehead and large almond eyes. The muzzle is small with large nostrils. It has a long neck, sloping shoulders and a slim body with deep girth. The coat is thin and fine, and the mane and tail fine and silky. The breed was believed to be extinct for a thousand years until it was rediscovered in the 1960s on the southern shores of the Caspian Sea by Louise Firouz, the American-born wife of an Iranian aristocrat, who chanced upon a stallion in the streets of a coastal market town. After DNA tests proved that she had found the lost breed, Firouz established a breeding programme to ensure its survival. The smallest horses reach only to their owners' waists, and their long, level paces, natural grace and balance make them suitable for dressage. In fact Caspian stallions were raced by children in jockey silks on Tehran's racetrack in the late 1960s.

Walster, who competes in dressage, started out in the hunting field, whipping in and working with hounds until she set up her own yard. 'We run on about 35 acres,' she notes. 'We slowly built up the stables, starting with just four and building them up as money allowed it. We put the yards in for the horses to live in as and when we were financially able … We just built on a dream, shall we say.' And has that dream been fulfilled? 'It can never end, a dream, can it? Walster says. 'I'd like to see the ponies out competing for Great Britain; that's probably my biggest aim. We've got ponies who are very close to it, but we still want them on the teams.'

The Caspian Horse (opposite) is a miniature equine beauty, equal in every way to its much larger Arabian purebred descendants. Although rare in Britain, several breeders, among them Penny Walster (left), have made it their life's work to preserve the breed, which only escaped extinction in the 1970s through the efforts of Louise Firouz in Iran, where the breed originated

Nikki & Bridget Brown

Endurance riders, Westerdale, North Yorkshire

Nikki and Bridget Brown's farm dates back at least as far as the era of the Knights Templar, with an abandoned monastery on the site of an Iron Age village. Mother Bridget and daughter Nikki run the farm together and take in rescue horses, which 'just seem to appear'; some have gone on to achieve high levels of endurance. The Browns currently have ten horses, including one Arabian stallion, as well as cows and sheep.

Nikki saved up to buy her first horse, Star, by breeding hamsters and guinea pigs at the age of six. 'To me,' she explains, 'endurance is about getting out there and seeing new places, and being with your best friend ... You have to know your horse, and you have to know what it can do and where its limits are, as well.' Some horses are better on hills while others excel on the flat, where speed is essential to success. Stages can be as long as 30 miles, but the distances decrease the further you ride. Bridget reminds her daughter that when she did the Cairngorm 100, the total daily distance was 100, the riding time was 16.5 hours, 'but the actual time to do the ride with the vet gates and everything was twenty-two hours.' Nikki remembers taking two horses up with her; a friend rode one while she rode the other. 'The one that I thought would struggle actually did better,' she says. 'She kept going and kept going, and when we got to the finish and there was all the lights and cars everywhere, you could feel her going, "Oh thank God, we've finished!" She lifted herself up and her ears pricked and she trotted straight through the middle of everybody. She was so chuffed – you could feel her being so happy.' Nikki admits to talking 'nonstop' when she is on a horse, or singing, 'which is really quite embarrassing!' She jokes that the horses' 'ears go back and they go, "Oh God!"'

Endurance GB, the sport's national governing body, is split into different groups throughout the country. The sport is 75 per cent women, half of whom are older. 'It's spending time with your horse,' explains Bridget of the sport's attraction. 'Endurance is anywhere between 10 miles and 100 miles in a day. There are several categories: pleasure rides, which is 10 to 20 miles; competitive, which is 20 to 50 miles; then there's endurance racing, which is 50 to 100 miles over a set course. The horses are vetted every 25 miles when they start competing. Very, very vigorously. There is little money to be made at lower levels of the sport, so most endurance riders do it for pleasure. Most mounts are Arabs, whether pure- or part-bred.' The Browns' stallion is purebred; his stud fee at the moment is £400. 'Hopefully when he's higher up and qualified – because he's not broken to ride yet – his stud fee will go up,' notes Bridget. Potentially he can do up to twenty coverings per year, with the proceeds going to 'back the farm up'.

Nikki observes that the toughest ride in the world is the Tevis Cup in America, '200 miles or something, and high up in the mountains'. 'We want to do the Tevis,' says her mother. 'The Cairngorm's based on the Tevis. That's why they ran it – somebody wanted a British equivalent.'

(opposite) Living at the second-highest point on the Yorkshire moors is a blessing or a curse, depending on whether you are a city person or a country diehard. Mother and daughter Nikki and Bridget Brown test that point to its limits on their small farm, with the clouds as their ceiling. Nikki (right) bought her first horse at the age of six with money saved from rearing hamsters

Sir Humphry Wakefield, Bt, FRGS

Horseman, explorer & antiquarian, Chillingham Castle, Alnwick, Northumberland

Born in London in 1936, Sir Humphry Wakefield lived in India up to the age of ten. Initially educated by a private tutor, he went to Gordonstoun and Cambridge, where he became interested in the arts. Sir Humphry has travelled widely; in 1990, he joined the New Zealand Everest expedition, and he survived a plane crash in the Antarctic. A passionate horseman who rides daily, he was a captain in the 10th Royal Hussars, serving in Jordan, Germany, Cyprus and Malta. He went on to work at Christie's in the Musical Instruments Department (during the 1960s), to be a Director of Mallet & Son, to create a Stately Homes Collection for Baker Furniture, and to purchase Chillingham Castle, which had fallen into such decay that the roof had caved in. With no estate of his own, he wanted to 'invent a Wakefield base from nothing' (his wife's family were descended from the Greys of Chillingham). The castle is open to the public six months of the year. 'I love opening to the public cos people come round and they love it, and they become friends, and if they don't love it, I quite like attacking them too,' Sir Humphry jokes. 'We've a wing which has rooms to rent out ... We have concerts, we have events ... It helps to make ends meet ... Chillingham Castle has always been a centre of interest or of activity, of arts and crafts, of riding horses, of shooting, of field sports, love of animals, all these things. It's been a sort of centre of happenings, and I'm the boss of it for this chapter.'

Sir Humphry remembers riding 5 miles every morning with his parents from the age of three-and-a-half. 'I love my sports,' he enthuses. 'I love, love, love my soldiery! I was a soldier in the Middle East, and that was fantastic. We wound up camping in Jordan for fourteen months ... We had tanks, but we had wonderful ponies. We got ponies from the Baghdad racecourse, and we played polo on them.' While based in New York for Mallet, he 'wandered the world selling things, and telling the factories how to make them, and correcting the factories, and finding the things and detailing them. That was a wonderful part of my life. I was riding horses throughout.' Meanwhile he was also indulging his passion for collecting: 'I'm like a magpie: collect, collect, collect.'

Will Sir Humphry ever give up riding? 'I hope not,' he says. 'A lot of my friends have had rather bad falls off their horses and that stops them riding, but I hope that the Almighty will look after me ... I've been incredibly lucky so far.' A segmented journey on horseback from John O'Groats to Land's End came about because he wanted to do some writing. 'I thought I might write about my life,' he explains. 'No-one will read about it, but it would get it off my chest, as it were ... So I thought what I'd do is set off riding and dictate as I went along ... But unfortunately, the moment you are on a horse, you forget about writing. You look at the stars, you look at the sky, you wonder where you should have your first bar of chocolate, and then you wonder where is a good place for lunch.' The arrangement he has with a travelling friend 'is very spoiling' in that the friend drives Sir Humphry's horsebox, 'and in that horsebox there's a bed, and after we've ridden 20 or 30 miles, we look for somewhere to stay'. The experience of riding across England has proven to him that 'one's not as busy as one thought one was. It proves to me that when you die, things will go on, that truly the most beautiful thing is nature. Purely. Art is wonderful and music is wonderful, but nature is more beautiful again ... You see a wonderful flower in a Dutch painting, but the flower itself is more wonderful again ... If you are in your tent at 5.00 in the morning, you open the flap and you see snowy mountains, you see streams, and you see sunlight, all of that, that's more beautiful again ... Riding through the hills, riding through everywhere, you get blasted with the glory of nature.' The companionship of a horse 'is perfect because he's a friend, and he keeps you moving around. He moves at just the right pace for you to look at nature ... If you are on a motorcycle or motorbike, you have to look where you are going; if you are walking, you have to look where you are going. If you are on a horse, the horse is looking where he's going, and you are just that right height off the ground to get an extra horizon ... You are nearer to God, you are looking down at the ground, you get a better perspective, you are moving at an all right pace for looking at things, and it's the whole glory of existence really. You suddenly don't want to write anything any more or do anything any more. You just want to ride and look at things.'

Sir Humphry Wakefield and his Friesian called Barack O'Bouncer (bred at his own stables) in the gardens of Chillingham Castle (right). Sir Humphry has been a keen rider since the age of six, having lived through more history and drama than most novelists can conjure. 'If you are on a horse ... you are nearer to God!' he exclaims

(following spread) The denuded, forbidding lunar landscapes of the Durham Dales – abandoned coal faces from the days of strip mining – reflect the baleful beauty left by humanity's plundering of nature

Albion Saddlemakers

Walsall, West Midlands

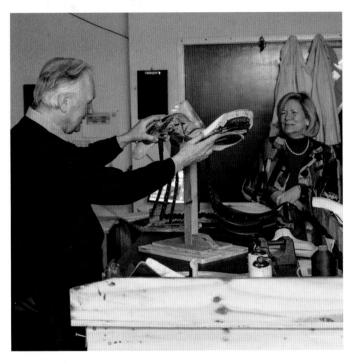

(above) Owner and founder Paul Belton, with his wife Sherry, measuring the balance of a saddle, something which is part-craftsmanship, part visual expertise. (above right) Tools of the saddlemaker's trade abandoned for a tea break. (opposite) The various intricate stages of the craft, culminating in the superbly finished product

Founded in 1985, Albion Saddlemakers is one of the world's leading saddle designers and manufacturers. Chairman Paul Belton studied design engineering and is an experienced rider, having worked with Ernst Bachinger in Vienna. Managing Director Sherry Belton also trained in Vienna, with the late dressage specialist Franz Rochowansky. The Beltons design, manufacture and supply competition saddles, bridles and accessories which maximise comfort and enhance performance. Their business has two offshoots: Albion Couture House, which produces bags and belts, and Albion Sporting, which offers gun slips, magazine cases and other products created with the couple's daughter Annie Belton and fellow Director Fin Green.

Paul explains that customers are attracted to Albion because 'they know there are so few sources, and it makes such a difference in the performance of the horse.' Saddlery, he notes, 'started in Walsall about two thousand years ago', with the invasion of the Romans, who found that water running underground from the Welsh hills filtered through limestone caverns before surfacing in Walsall. 'This made the water exceptionally good for preparing leather for saddlery,' he says. When Paul returned to England from Vienna, he found that 'dressage trainers were basically dying of starvation. There was no work'. After

doing 'whatever work' he could find, he decided to convert his experience into the creation of performance-enhancing products: 'I initially had other people manufacturing for me, but then, because I wanted to get first-hand experience of the skills of creating the products, I had to come to Walsall, because this was the key centre of knowledge for the whole of the UK.'

Sherry Belton worked as a systems analyst, but her 'passion was riding ... Eventually I started working with Paul; he was producing saddles and I was selling them ... Then I became a freelance saddle fitter'. Although there are about thirty saddlemakers in England, 'what makes us different', explains Sherry, 'is we have a fundamental grounding in equestrianism, and we understand what the horse and the rider need to work together in harmony. Harmony is the most difficult part of the relationship to create because you are asking a rider to sit on a horse that moves in a different way to the way the human walks'. When asked to name the world's best saddle, Sherry replies, 'One of our sponsored riders, William Fox-Pitt, will say his best saddle is an Albion lightweight saddle because it stopped him breaking his neck when he fell off at Burghley ... It's down to personal choice, and everybody wants to feel something different.'

(left) A winter wonderland on Exmoor in Somerset, with a wild Exmoor pony foraging for food oblivious to the beautiful surroundings

Piggy French

Eventer & breeder, Maidwell, Northamptonshire

Piggy French's mother evented and produced horses to advanced level. Watching her competing is what inspired French to ride herself. Having considered a career in art, she abandoned her course after a term when she discovered she could not live without being able to compete – and that involved riding. Today one of Britain's leading eventers, French has a long list of wins and placings to her credit. She has been a team member for Great Britain at world and European championships, won the individual silver medal at the 2009 European Eventing Championships at Fontainebleau, and in 2010 represented Britain as an individual in the World Equestrian Games in Kentucky. She was selected in 2017 to represent Team GB at the FEI European Eventing Championships in Strzegom. Her best result that year was second place at Burghley 4-star level.

The custom-designed March Stud was established by French and her partner Tom March, with whom she has worked since 2012. The couple breed, compete and sell outstanding equine athletes for top-level equestrian sports. French describes her obsession with 'working with horses,

(left) Piggy French putting a horse to stable at the end of a hard day's work, having started at 6.00 a.m. and finished at 6.00 p.m. (opposite) French in a moment of reflection riding an Irish Sport Horse called Cooley Monsoon, owned by Ab Fab comedian Jennifer Saunders

improving horses, getting the very best out of them' this way: 'If they do really well, I love that even more. I suppose to win is a massive part; I'm disappointed if I don't win because I've messed up in my training or my riding ability for that competition. If I've not ridden the horse quite well enough or I've messed up, it really irritates me.' She cites patience and a 'tough, tough skin' as being critical to success.

Eventing, French explains, is more complicated, if not more demanding, than other equine sports. 'You're training for three different things,' she notes. 'The hours that you would have to spend with each horse to get them fit enough to train, the dressage, to teach them to go cross-country – and ... it's a high-risk sport as well. You have to get quite intimate with the horse for our game, because to get a horse to be top and very successful is a bit of a getting into their minds as well. You have to really train them in so many different ways, whereas in racing you've got the trainer who trains the horse, but the jockey gets on for the moment and does that bit ... You've got to be hungry and very brave and fearless for when you go round the big tracks.'

French's great regret is to have missed out on the 2012 London Olympics, for which she had been selected with two horses, only to have both of them injured. 'It was an absolute killer,' she remembers. 'My dad owned half of the two horses that I was taking to the Olympics with a very good friend of his that's supported me for five or six years. We didn't go out and buy Olympic horses ... We made them ... It was a fucking disaster to be honest, on every level. Sponsors went, owners went; they thought their horse was next to be injured ... [But] you can't wrap them up in cotton wool and leave them in their stables to get to the Olympics. They're athletes; they need to be getting fit.'

'I'm a very private person, but I live for my animals,' concludes French. 'You have to go back and start making the next horses come up, which takes a long time ... I was desperate for team gold; I thought it could be doable, and I thought either one of the horses going the best that they could do, could have been good enough for individual ... I don't think with horses you can think, That's going to happen, because they throw so much at you the whole time and there's such a fine line between it being brilliant or crap! It's just staying focused to try and stay above that line.'

Bicester Hunt with Whaddon Chase

Bicester, Oxfordshire

The Bicester Hunt, which can trace its history back two hundred years, was re-formed from an amalgamation of the Bicester & Warden Hill and the Whaddon Chase at the start of the 1986–7 season. Under the chairmanship of Peter Rymer, the hunt is governed by a committee that authorises the Masters to manage its affairs. Rules of conduct include operating only with the full cooperation of landowners. The old Whaddon country is noted for its good scenting ground, while the North End is supported by a farming community which enjoys its hunting in a largely unspoiled landscape.

Hunt member and former model Lady Martha Sitwell founded habit-design company Sitwell & Whippet and is the creator of a gin blend, Martha's Marvellous Jumping Juice, 20 per cent of whose sales proceeds go to spinal research. Along with other family members, she trekked across Mongolia to honour her sister Polly's memory and raise money for the mental-health charity Mind. Having broken her neck and back in a bad crash off a horse as a teenager, Sitwell found that riding side-saddle was a way back into riding.

'We're not allowed to hunt foxes anymore so we go trail hunting,' explains Sitwell. 'A nice chap goes off on a horse in the morning, and he's got a rag dipped in God knows what, but it's meant to emulate the scent of a fox.' While she especially loves to watch hounds work, Sitwell notes that 'there's a bond that you build with your horse out hunting that you can't build any other way ... But also I love to be in nature ... You get to ride across pieces of land that you would never ordinarily get to see.' Sitwell's friend Lucy Holland, a Master of the Bicester Hunt, organised the first Silver Spur Challenge hunt ride – a traditional steeplechase run over 2½ miles of grassland with twenty hedges to jump – in 2016. Sitwell calls her 'one of the greatest horsewomen of I don't know how many generations ... because most of the horses that she has are given to her because nobody else can ride them. She'll take them and, I don't know, she's like a horse magician; her affinity with nature is kind of magical ... For the hunting, she goes around and speaks to all the farmers beforehand and says, "This is where we'd like to come," and the farmer will say, "Okay, you can go in this field, but you can't go in this field" ... The farmers really get nothing out of it. The hounds eat the fallen stock'. By 'fallen stock' is meant a cow that has broken a leg and has to be shot or old horses that have been put down. Holland extols fox hunting as 'by far the most ecologically sound way of controlling a population that needs to be controlled ... The other beauty of fox hunting, when we were permitted to [do it], is that the fox is either dead or alive. At no point is it wounded and suffering ... Foxes are beautiful – I love foxes – but I do realise that they need to be controlled'.

Holland notes that about half of English hunts have women as Masters, so she is not an anomaly. The schedule she oversees is punishing: 'We hunt four days a week, but we also hunt a dog pack and a bitch pack. Not many people do that; most people mix the dogs and the bitches ... We normally start autumn hunting in September, and that is sometimes up to six times a week ... We finish the second week of March, Cheltenham week ... We leave the meet at about 11.15 a.m., and we normally finish when it's dark.' She adds that different people 'get different things from it ... For people who hunt a lot, it's all about watching the hounds work. When they're hunting really well, it's the most exciting thing in the world'. The breeding of hounds goes back hundreds of years, Holland notes. 'There's a book called *Baily's [Hunting Directory]* and it has all the hound breeding in it ... [Sometimes] we use other people's stallion hounds. That's one of their best hounds, or one that's compatible to what we're breeding.' Hounds are exchanged between hunts, never sold: 'Some hunts don't breed their own hounds, some only ever draft hounds in ... For example, we have two or three hounds that like chasing deer, which is a problem because we've got a lot of deer. Those would go to an area that doesn't have a lot of deer [and] that hunt would get an interesting bloodline.'

(opposite) Lucy Holland,
Master of the Hunt,
discussing strategy with
her huntsman Guy Allman.
(right) Lady Martha Sitwell,
a longtime fox-hunting
aficionado, rides side-saddle
through every form of
challenging countryside,
including fences and
other obstacles. 'We're not
allowed to hunt foxes any
more so we go trail hunting,'
she explains

(above left) Simon Holland (centre) alongside Lady Martha Sitwell, toasting fellow adventurers fortified by port and the anticipation of a hard ride. (above) Sarah Byrne, social stylist and a longtime side-saddle rider possessed of elegant poise. (opposite) Melanie Pejkovic shows how it's done, a glass of port in hand for toasting (or mustering) courage

(following spread) Members of the Bicester Hunt gather at Kirtlington Park, Oxfordshire

Alex Fenton & Jason Wood

Travellers, Kirtlington, Oxfordshire

'A traveller is a cultural thing to a lot of people,' observes Alex Fenton. 'In this country we have Romany travellers, Irish travellers, then I suppose New Age travellers, who weren't born travellers but chose the lifestyle.' 'Then you've got the second generation: kids that have been on the road from the '70s when their parents were going to festivals ... The children have carried on and had children themselves,' adds Jason Wood. 'Every single person that lives in a bus or a wagon or a lorry or a caravan, they've all got different tales to tell of why they're on the road.' Wood describes himself as a 'gorger' – 'someone that was born and bred in a house'.

Fenton and Wood's horses are both Gypsy Cobs, which, as Wood explains, 'were bred by Gypsies to pull wagons. Originally, you had big Shires and Clydesdales, too big for wagons. So what they did at the turn of the century was start to breed all these big English and Scottish working horses with small, traditional English native ponies ... A Gypsy Cob ... was hardy to live on the side of the road and eat natural things'. Also called 'Irish Cobs', 'Gypsy Horses' or 'Gypsy Vanners', these horses are small and solidly built, piebald or skewbald, and possess flowing manes and tails and feathered heels. Gentle and tractable by nature, they were only recently recognised as a distinct breed.

Wood made the decision to go travelling after 'going to Castle Morton in 1992, which was the biggest free festival in England we've ever had, fifty thousand people ... We had a massive rave ... I've recently got into horses because in this country, with the New Age traveller scene as with all the more traditional people who wanted to be different, the authorities ... realised, "Hold on, if we carry on evicting these people, they'll carry on moving. If we stop evicting and let them settle, they'll naturally do that."' Oxfordshire Council runs six permanent sites for travellers; there are twenty-one privately run sites in the county as well. The Council has a duty of care to all Gypsies and travellers within the county and conducts negotiations between the traveller and settled communities.

Fenton, a tree surgeon by trade, notes that travelling is not a carefree lifestyle, especially when it turns cold, wet and muddy. 'But you toughen up quite quickly,' she says. 'You make sure you've got plenty of fuel.' Living outdoors, she adds, is 'healthier; living simply, with less, is very satisfying. It's needing less out of life'. The greatest plus: 'Walking down the road with your horse – that freedom. People that live in houses, if you don't get on with your neighbour, if you have problems, you're stuck there.'

(left) Jason Wood with his Gypsy Cob called Tank and his dog, waiting for the Bicester Hunt to move back into action in adjoining fields. 'Live and let live' is Wood's philosophy about hunting: 'They're not pushing us out of their posh neighbourhood.' (opposite) Wood and Alex Fenton, with her horse Rebel, preparing their mounts for the night. 'The feel of the hunters' horses galloping past always gives me a great buzz,' Fenton says

The Welsh bank of the River Wye in winter flood (left), by (opposite) the twelfth-century ruins of Kintern Abbey in Monmouthshire

The Welsh Cob

Bev & Jonathan Batt, Breeders, Abergavenny, Monmouthshire

Bev and Jonathan Batt in their stable yard (above), and (opposite) their splendid twelve-year-old Welsh Cob mare Abergavenny Valmai

Abergavenny Stud was founded in 1980, initially with the Ffynonwen prefix. The first Welsh Cob bred there was Ffynonwen Alexis, born in 1984. Since that time, the stud has grown in size to two Welsh Cob stallions and twenty mares. Bev Batt claims the oldest family connection with the Welsh Cob; her grandfather Lloyd Prosser kept them. Both Batt children are also involved with the breed.

The Welsh Cob is first mentioned in the laws of Hywel Dda, the tenth-century ruler of Deheubarth (southern Wales). By the fifteenth century, the breed was well established, and around two hundred years later it began to be used by farmers. Strong enough to carry an adult but calm enough to carry a child, the breed is known for its courage, intelligence and natural ability to jump, which make Welsh Cobs ideal hunters for rough or hilly country. Likely brought to Britain by the Romans from their African campaigns and abandoned when they withdrew in AD 410, there are four types of Welsh Cobs and ponies. 'There's the Section A,' explains Jonathan, 'which is predominantly the child's, the lead-rein pony; the Section B, which is a bit bigger, a little more refined, which is the child's pony, a slightly older child; then you have the Section C; and then you have the Section D, which is the Welsh Cob.' He goes on to explain that the breed's attraction abroad is down to their being all-rounders, 'so they may have less in numbers, but they do more'. In fact they make good hunters when crossed with a thoroughbred or another breed. 'What you used to find is that if you took the Welsh Cob hunting, it would be very hardy – you wouldn't have any going lame or things like that – but would it have the staying power of a thoroughbred or something, to be out all day with the hounds, maybe not,' muses Jonathan. 'What people have done more and more over the last twenty or thirty years, they've crossed them with a thoroughbred, so they've got the hardiness in the legs and the strength of a Cob, but then they've got the athleticism of a thoroughbred or a warmblood. So they're crossing with both, but they want the strength of those bones.' Describing her ideal Welsh Cob, Bev lists 'a nice big, bold eye, small ears, a pretty head, not pretty like an Arab but a nice-quality head with a nice jawline ... It's got to be quality first'.

Alex & Melissa Hickey

Managers, Snowdonia Riding Stables, Caernarfon, Snowdonia

'Working with horses is a way of life. I can't imagine going and sitting in an office every day,' says Melissa Hickey, who, together with Alex Hickey, runs Snowdonia Riding Stables. 'A large majority of what we do is trekking, so we take people out for rides, but we also train people to ride ... Then we do hacking on young horses, problem horses, during the winter months ... It's just a way of life, and although we don't earn millions and millions of pounds, we earn enough to have a happy life and to enjoy ourselves and still do what we love.'

Snowdonia National Park in North Wales sees a lot of tourism, especially during the summer; Snowdon, the highest peak in Wales and England, is a magnet for climbers. 'We don't have to have rights and access,' Melissa notes of the park. 'It's just free for us to go up and explore.' Most of their horses are 'Cob crosses, Welsh Mountain ponies, thoroughbred crosses, a couple of half-Shires, Gypsy Vanners'. All of them must be 'really hardy horses because they're going out onto the mountain so they've got to be really sure-footed. We can't buy a load of Arabs and take them up the mountain; they wouldn't be able to deal with the terrain, it's too rocky. We need strong, solid, steady horses. That's why we go for the cross-breeds usually. Not just for their ability – they have stamina to go up the terrain – but also their carefulness'. As members of the British Horse Society, Melissa and Alex are obliged to put their horses' welfare first, which involves 'making sure the horses are fit for use and purpose'. As Melissa explains, 'They are taken very good care of in this country. I have been to other countries but chose never to ride because a lot of people don't have that help to maintain the horses.'

(left) Alex and Mel Hickey on morning stable duty at Snowdonia Riding Stables. (right) A group of riders contemplating the risk of fording the River Afon Gwyrfai in full flow

(following spread) A stupendous multi-coloured landscape encountered while crossing Snowdonia National Park in Wales

The Cleveland Bay

Sally & Brian Comb, Breeders, Castlerise Stud, Bedfordshire

The family-run Castlerise Stud has been in business for nearly fifty years, with a focus on the Cleveland Bay. The Combs breed from 'well-established, quality bloodlines' of Cleveland Bay and Irish Draught horses on about 80 acres.

The Cleveland Bay is England's oldest breed, having originated in the Cleveland area of Yorkshire. Incredibly versatile and used for multiple disciplines, the breed is thought to have evolved from crossing native bay-coloured mares with Oriental stallions during the 1600s. A breed of durability, longevity and quiet disposition, the characteristic black legs, mane and tail are *de rigeur*, and the horses' feet must be blue in colour. Developed as hunters, coach or pack horses and agricultural workers, the breed came under threat with the arrival of the railways. By the 1880s, the Cleveland Bay was on the verge of extinction, and by the early 1960s, there were only a handful of mature stallions in England. The breed's resurgence is credited in part to HM The Queen, who purchased a purebred named Mulgrave Supreme and made the horse available at a public stud. 'She still actually breeds Clevelands,' Sally Comb notes, 'and she has them for her coaching horses ... The Queen always has her greys, but the rest of the royal family use [Cleveland Bays] on their carriages at Ascot, royal parades, anything that's going up the Mall.'

'We've only got thirty-three breeding mares left in the country now,' Sally goes on to explain, 'and there's a reluctance by some mare owners to actually put their mares in foal ... Not everybody has the facilities.' It was Sally's parents who established the stud: 'My parents were very old-school. My father worked with his grandfather who has horse buses in Newton, so I've been brought up virtually with horses.' She notes that 'up to about twenty years ago, everyone thought that a good Cleveland cross was the best hunting horse you could get. It then evolved that everybody wanted the thoroughbreds, the lightweights, because they were faster, they were quicker, but now it's gradually going back that they want something again that's got a little bit of substance.'

Sally's husband Brian, who used to show-jump, is in charge of the yard. 'I do all the horses, I cover the mares, I do all the stud work,' he explains. The couple have about fifty horses on the premises. 'We haven't lost one of the Cleveland foals, touch wood,' Brian notes. 'But I think the best thing that has happened to us is our young stallion,' adds Sally. 'We saw him in June last year and he was a horrible, messy, muddy ball of fluff stood in a field. We looked at him and thought, There's something about him ... We were warned off him by several people ... but we ... brought him home. The first show we took him to, he was the Young Stock champion, the Breed Champion and then the Overall Champion. Then we took him to the Rare Breed of the Year Show and he was the Rare Breed of the Year Cleveland Champion as well!'

(far left) Brian Comb exercising his prize Cleveland Bay horse Wyevale Wot a Charmer in the winter sun. (left) The stables at Castlerise Stud. (opposite) The splendid figure of Hallhouse Gladimere basking in welcome winter sunshine

The Cheltenham Festival

Cheltenham, Gloucestershire

The fashionable Victorian spa town of Cheltenham on the edge of the Cotswolds is known principally for the steeplechase races held there every March. Steeplechasing began in Ireland in the 1700s, the same period during which racing began at Cheltenham. Race events were characterised by extravagant parties, sideshows, and drinking and gambling booths, catering to every class of visitor. At one point, the prevalence of pickpockets, drunkards, card sharps and prostitutes caused the race meeting to be disrupted; the following year, the facilities were burned to the ground. From 1830, the venue was moved to Prestbury Park for flat racing, but the ground proved too soggy, so the event was shifted back up the hill. Cheltenham Racecourse founder W. A. Baring Bingham purchased the site with the intention of reviving the facilities and using the park as a stud farm. The first National Hunt Festival was held in 1902.

Frederick Cathcart, clerk of the course at the beginning of the twentieth century and founding Chairman of The Steeplechase Company Ltd, proposed that Cheltenham should focus on a particular discipline, as Newmarket had done with flat racing. Prize money began at £815. The event was expanded to three days in 1927, and the following year saw the extended 3-mile steeplechase, the Cheltenham Gold Cup. After Cathcart died, the racecourse was bought by Johnny Henderson, late father of trainer Nicky Henderson; he and his City friends formed Racecourse Holdings Trust. This prompted massive investment, with the BBC embracing racing as a key element of its broadcast agenda. In 1964 Racecourse Holdings Trust (renamed Jockey Club Racecourses) was formed to secure Cheltenham's future. Today the group owns thirteen other racecourses, a combination of jump, flat, dual-purpose and all-weather courses. Overall, it is owned by The Jockey Club.

The festival is now the county's biggest single revenue-earning event, generating an estimated £50 million for local hotels, shops, pubs and clubs. The year 2005 marked the first four-day festival with six races on each day. The first four-day festival was undoubtedly a huge success, and the format was retained in 2006 and looks set to stay. Well over two hundred thousand spectators attend over the four days. Friday is now Gold Cup day, with the Triumph Hurdle, Foxhunters and County Hurdle still appearing on the final afternoon. A new Cheltenham Gold Cup is minted each year. With ticket prices ranging from £20 to £80, the estimated gate receipts total around £7 million. Today, prize money at the festival is almost £3.4 million, an amazing average of roughly £125,000 per race, with around half of that total coming from sponsors.

(opposite left) Picnic tables, brogues, fanciful hats and country fare celebrating the horse alongside the West Country social scene. Cheltenham is considered the most 'people-friendly' of events in the British racing calendar, with loud bookies (opposite right) animating the ceremonies. (right) 'Flight of Fancy' should have been the name of the winning horse displayed on the screen behind the feathered splendour of a lady's hat!

(right) Jockeys at fence 15 are outnumbered by the private helicopters that come and go during the Cheltenham Festival. (below) The intense emotions of a true enthusiast are obvious in the face of a woman looking for fortune in the racing booklet on Champion Day. (opposite) The statuesque figure of a jockey with his frieze-like mount among the crowd too focused on betting to notice the horse's polished hooves and jockey's chiselled face as they dance towards the starters' box

(left) The equine journey
ends against a magnificent
Cotswolds backdrop,
following a quest across
a nation rooted in history
and traditions as old and
strong as the limestone
making up the wall

Acknowledgements

Every journey has a beginning and an end, but I can't readily put my finger on the beguine of the beginning for *Equine Journeys: The British Horse World*. My fascination with the subject of *Equus* dates back to early school days, whetted by a bookworm's voracious appetite for reading history (which repeatedly brings the virtual traveller back to the reality and importance of the horse) and a search for the origins of humanity's quest for freedom as expressed through speed and the exhilaration of wild danger, fashioned by its lust for battle and conquest.

Times have changed, but the urge for excellence endures in horsemanship and the public taste for speed. Quenching this personal thirst for adventure in creative knowledge, the exploration of the exotic in spatial settings, and the erotic in the intellectual sense of the word, has driven my own race against the cycle of the seasons (and time's limiting possibilities), resulting in my undertaking another book about horses. Having already experienced an exotic journey in a quest for the Arabian breed twenty years ago, my first thanks should embrace *The Arabian Horse*, initially published in 1998. An urge to do a sequel decided me on *Equine Journeys*. Someone who has been a side-saddle companion to the project these last few years is Caroline Campkin, whose patience and endurance have been tested not only by my Mongolian traits but also by the challenge of ill-health. Jamie Camplin, an old friend, and publisher of *The Arabian Horse*, cast the initial editorial master's eye which has served to focus my wandering one. In bringing vision to reality, no-one has been as instrumental as Roger Fawcett-Tang, my long-time mule trader in creative design. Roger is deserving of the red rosette, to borrow the parlance of the horse world. Different-coloured prize rosettes go to my core editorial team: Andrea Belloli, Consulting Editor; Anne Field, Project Director; and Emily Bryson, Project Coordinator. Andrea's editorial and writing skills are amplified by the book's achievements in such a short space of time. Anne's attention to research and editorial detail is always welcome. Young Emily learned to jump through hoops to get what was needed by demanding tribunes and survived up to the last hurdle. Liz Jones is owed gratitude for her proofreading. The publishers wish also to thank Lauren Nicole Collins, Rachel Horsman, Catriona Montgomery and Xaviera Alvarez Nordström for transcription services.

This is the first book where I've undertaken all of the photography – a challenging task at the best of times but nothing compared to the doubly exhausting enterprise of driving across Britain in pursuit of the horse, its keepers, breeders and dreamers, in order to interview and photograph those featured in the book. Several other worthy picture-makers were engaged along the way for fun and flavour. Maryam Homayoun Eisler contributed worthy photography (pp. 198, 204–5, 272–3, 314, 315, 317) along with her aesthetic sensibility and a keen eye for the killer shot. Kit Houghton contributed, when time and circumstances disallowed my own presence, the fairy-tale image of Exmoor bathed in snow (p. 292), plus Badminton's mad horses'-and-Englishmen's (and -women's) parade of guts and glory (pp. 82–3). The Jockey Club (pp. 56–7) and Tattersalls (pp. 74–5) kindly provided complementary imagery to fill the spaces that time, weather and fatigue did not permit me to fill.

My thanks to Christopher Joll for his fine essay on the history of the British horse, and for his learned equine counsel. Thames & Hudson, my long-time co-publishers, are thanked; while particular gratitude is extended to Eric Ladd and XY Digital for their excellent colour separation work and Imago.

Special thanks are due to Lt Gen Sir Barnabas White-Spunner and Lord Patrick Beresford for their initial support, guidance and advice; Sir Humphry Wakefield and Lady Martha Sitwell for background directions; Willow Kemp and Alexandra Homan for early support of the project; Arabella Morris Oppenheimer for her dedication to her sport and our project; Anthony Ernest Oppenheimer for his time; Lady Alison Myners, Lila Pearson, Major Patrick Waygood, Liz Higgin and Diana Butler; Sir Mark Prescott, William Butler, Richard Brown and Simon Crisford for their Newmarket nous; Nicky Henderson, Oliver Sherwood and Kim Bailey for their National Hunt expertise; Capt Ian Farquhar, Jo Aldridge and Lucy Holland for their help with leading fox hunts; John, Carolyn and Jake Warren for their unique perspectives on thoroughbred breeding; Michael Whitaker and Mary King for eventing; Deidre Hyde and Linda Grosse, Gerard Naprous and Misdee Wright Miller; and Lady Sabina and Lord St John of Bletso for kindness and support. And Sofia Cisneros Solares for small inspirations.

Last, yet topping the list, are the profilees – individuals and organisations who took time and care to ensure our effective coverage of their studs, horse farms, stables and all things horsey: they're the principal heroes of the book.

The publishers would also like to express their gratitude to the numerous other worthy participants in, and contributors to, the book, including Mohammed Al Habtoor, Guy Allman, Claire Allmett, Bridget Andrews, Darcie Asprey, Bev and Jonathan Batt, Michael Bell, Paul and Sherry Belton, Susan Booth, Bridget and Nikki Brown, Sarah Byrne, Bettina Bonnefoy, Ewen Cameron, Henry Carnall, Maddy Collins, Brian and Sally Comb, Grizelda Cowan, Oliver Cudmore, Jessica Dalgleish, Ben Elery, Lilly Elizabeth, Nick Gauntlett, Jimmy George, Steven Golding, Mary Griffiths, Charlie Hanbury, Kate Hanson, Mahtab Hanjani, Will Harper, Alex Hickey, Mel Hickey, Edward Hitchman, Simon Holland, Emma Hooley, Nick and Celina Hopkins, Chris Hyde, Roisin Kinney, Tim Lane, Dayna Lee, Caroline Llewellyn, Jemma and James Lucas, Ben Maher, Nina Marsh, Fi Mitchell, Isabelle Moore, Ailsa Noble, George Pearson, Melanie Pejkovic, Melita Peters, Tracy Petitt, Hayden Prince, Farzin Pourmokhtar, Trish Richards, Marilyn Scudamore, Julian Seaman, Billy Sheen, Harry Sleigh, Neil Starsmore, Iona Stokes, Emma Thorley, Kate Tierney, David and Emma Wallace, Ella Willshaw, and so many others who befriended the project along the way.

Hossein Amirsadeghi
London, July 2018